A TASTE OF LONDON

A TASTE OF LONDON

TRADITIONAL FOOD

BY THEODORA FITZGIBBON

Period photographs specially prepared by GEORGE MORRISON

1975 · HOUGHTON MIFFLIN COMPANY BOSTON

Library of Congress Cataloging in Publication Data
FitzGibbon, Theodora.
A taste of London.
Includes index.
1. Cookery, English.   2. London—Description—Views.
I. Title.
TX717.F393   1975   641.5′9421   75-5604
ISBN 0-395-20714-2

Printed in the United States of America

W 10 9 8 7 6 5 4 3 2 1

For all my friends who have helped me with
this book, but particularly for my friend from
childhood, Sophie: also John and Munko Orbach,
with love and many thanks.

ACKNOWLEDGMENTS

We both want to thank the many friends, both in London and elsewhere, who have helped us in the research for this book, particularly Miss Aileen Hamilton for the loan of many out-of-print books; Mrs Vera Orbach and Miss Roisin Kirwan, both of whom went to great trouble, and supplied valuable information; Mr J. G. Links for allowing us to use his collection of vivid photographs; my aunt, Mrs Florence Barden, who helped in so many ways while we were in London, and also Mr and Mrs John Orbach for their most kind hospitality.

We also wish to thank the following people for their kindness and help in the preparation of this book.

Miss Patricia Meara of Chelsea Public Library, who went to immense trouble for us; Mr Tony Allen of Rules Restaurant for recipes and information; Miss R. Watson, Photograph Librarian of the Greater London Council for her kind co-operation; Mrs Tuck and Miss S. Basinger of London Transport for supplying valuable details; Mr Peter Castle and Mr Christopher Hobbs of the Victoria and Albert Museum; Mr Howgego and Mr R. Hyde of the Guildhall Library for their help; Mr B. Curle of Kensington Public Library; Mr H. Davis and Mr J. Watson of the Local History Section of Greenwich Public Library, who were most helpful; Mrs C. Bayliss of Fulham and Hammersmith Central Libraries for finding us rare photographs and going to a great deal of trouble on our behalf; Dr D. Thomas and Mr J. Ward of the Science Museum, who gave freely of their valuable time; Mr Ricard of Swiss Cottage Library, who was most helpful. Also, many thanks to Mr C. Sorenson and Mrs S. Kington of the London Museum; Mrs Greening of the Port of London Authority; Mrs F. M. Rushton of the Radio Times Hulton Picture Library; Mr Stephen Croad, National Monuments Record; B. T. Batsford Ltd; Mr Helmut Gernsheim for his kindness in allowing us to use the photograph on page 55; also Mr William Gordon Davis for the photograph on page 41.

Photographs on pages xii (Spurgeon Collection), 2, 70 (Spurgeon Collection) are reproduced by kind permission of Greenwich Public Library; on pages 4, 8, 10, 12, 31 by kind permission of the Victoria and Albert Museum; on pages 6, 23, 79, 99, 116 by kind permission of Chelsea Public Library; on pages 14, 48, 102 by kind permission of the National Monuments Record; on pages 17, 24, 68 by kind permission of Swiss Cottage Public Library; on pages 26, 33, 73, 87, 112 by kind permission of Trustees of the London Museum; on pages 36, 38, 44, 46, 52, 62, 74, 76, 92, 99, 108, 114 by kind permission of the Guildhall Library; on pages 34, 65 by kind permission of Kensington Public Library; on page 29 by kind permission of London Transport; on pages 56, 58, 66, 83, 89, 106, 110 by kind permission of Hammersmith Public Library; on page 50 by kind permission of the Greater London Council; on page 60 by kind permission of the Science Museum; on pages 19, 119 by kind permission of the Radio Times Hulton Picture Library; on page 94 by kind permission of Westminster Public Library; on page 105 by kind permission of the Port of London Authority; on page 85 by kind permission of B. T. Batsford Ltd; on page 91 by kind permission of *The Tatler*; on page 42 by kind permission of J. G. Links Esquire; on page 80 by kind permission of Mrs C. S. Monson; on page 55 by kind permission of Mr Helmut Gernsheim.

CONTENTS

Endpaper photographs by George Morrison, from original
drawings by Richard Doyle, 1849.
    front: Society enjoying itself at a Soiree!
    back: Showing the public dining on Whitebait, at
           Blackwall.

INTRODUCTION

London is thought to be a Celtic place-name, derived from the Celtic personal name of *Londinos*: other theories advanced are that the name is a Gaelic compound, i.e. 'Lon' being a plain, and 'Dun' or 'Don' an eminence or hill. Thomas Pennant writing in 1793 acknowledges William Owen of Barmouth's suggestion that it was derived from the Celtic 'Llyn Din' the lake fort. This theory is still supported. Whatever its origins, London has been a place of importance, and a capital city since Elizabethan times. It is a huge, sprawling, complex place and has seemed so to its inhabitants for several centuries. However, it is difficult to live there for any length of time without thinking of the poet Shelley's words: '. . . Yet in its depth what treasures!'

In the eighteenth century George Colman wrote:

> *Oh, London is a fine town,*
> *A very famous city,*
> *Where all the streets are paved with gold,*
> *And all the maidens pretty.*

This is still firmly believed by millions of people, which is why London is the clearing-house of the world, and contains so many ethnic groups. These groups, whether they be Jewish, Irish, Welsh (at one time most of the dairies in London were owned by Welshmen from Cardiganshire, known as 'Cardis') or Scottish, founded their own communities, keeping up their own traditions, yet at the same time becoming 'Londoners'. This also applied to the large numbers of Italians who settled mostly around Clerkenwell in London during the Risorgimento, bringing with them their gaily painted ice-cream carts, and barrel-organs. The 'hokey-pokey' man selling his ice-cream was a well loved figure. (The name is thought to have come from his original street-cry, 'ecco un poco'.) The mixture of Asiatic races in Dockland; the cosmopolitan atmosphere of Soho; the warmhearted and cheerful Cockney, all play their part in this great pageant which is London. The people are as important as the buildings, so throughout this book you will see the faces of the people who worked, lived and loved in nineteenth and early twentieth century London.

The food was as varied as the people and it is interesting to note that well-known French chefs such as Escoffier spent his entire working life in London at the Carlton and Savoy Hotels. Monsieur Ude, *ci-devant* chef to Louis XVI, who lived and worked here during and after the French Revolution said: 'I will venture to affirm that cookery in England when well done is superior to that of any country in the world.' Brillat-Savarin stayed for a time in England, also the Marquis d'Albignac. They both made quite a good living from starting the fashion of going to the big London houses, to 'dress' the salads. It is from this time that the English aristocracy assumed the French habit of dropping 'h's'; to say 'erbs, and 'otels was U speech in those days. Now, the habit has lapsed and only remains with the ill-educated. Alexis Soyer, famous chef of the Reform Club (see page 5), also had time to assist in the great Irish famine and to invent the field kitchen for army catering in the Crimea, as well as to write many books which are extremely practical for use today.

However, not all the well-known chefs were foreign, for

John Farley was principal cook of the famous London Tavern, which was the prototype for the first public restaurant opened in Paris by Antoine Beauvilliers in 1782. It was called 'Grande Taverne de Londres' and specialized in such dishes as 'plumbuting' and 'woueche rabette' as well as 'le rosbif'. Beauvilliers later wrote a cookery book and described his dishes as the 'best English cooking'.

All these factors are reflected in the food of London which is as varied as its inhabitants and its history. You will find here practical, everyday dishes, which are perhaps a little different. As I have said elsewhere, it is worth remembering that garlic, saffron, mace, cinnamon and many other spices and herbs were constantly used, centuries before the arrival of Indian tea in London, and this little book will show how they were used by the people portrayed in these pages.

THEODORA FITZGIBBON, 1972

Deilginis,   Dalkey,
Baile Átha Cliath.   Dublin.

'London—opulent, enlarged and still
Increasing LONDON—Babylon of old
Not more the glory of the earth than she.
A more accomplish'd world's chief glory now!
The villas with which London stands begirt
Like a swarth Indian with his belt of beads,
PROVE IT!'

William Cowper, 1731-1800

'Forget six counties overhung with smoke,
Forget the snorting steam and piston stroke,
Forget the spreading of the hideous town;
Think rather of the pack-horse on the down,
And dream of London, small and white and clean,
The clear Thames bordered by its gardens green.'

Prologue; *The Wanderers*, William Morris, 1834-96

PPLE FRITTERS

'A little old woman her living she got
By selling hot codlings* hot, hot, hot;
And this little old woman who codlings sold
Though her codlings were hot, she felt herself cold,
So to keep herself warm she thought it no sin
To fetch for herself a quartern of —
Ri tol iddy iddy, ri tol iddy iddy ri tol lay.'

Grimaldi's best remembered song, words by T. Dibdin; music
by John Whitaker

*Codlings are a variety of apple

APPLE FRITTERS

From *The Kitchen Oracle of Modern Culinary Art* by Samuel
Hobbs, *c.* 1886. Samuel Hobbs was a well known chef of the
'90s and cooked for all the best houses in London. Queen
Victoria sent a message to him saying that 'he had dressed the
best dinner the Queen of England had ever sat down to'.

FOR THE BATTER—about which Hobbs wrote 'it will always eat
crisp and requires no whipped white of eggs to be added to the
same. It is excellent too, for fish and other savoury uses'.

1 lb. (4 cups) (454 gr.) sifted flour	¼ pint (½ cup) (0·142 l.) salad oil
1 egg-yolk	grated rind of 1 lemon
½ pint (1 cup) (0·285 l.) light ale	warm sugar for finishing
10 medium sized apples	
deep fryer of oil	

Street sellers in Borough High Street, 1887.

'First make the batter by putting the sifted flour into a large
basin, add the egg-yolk and half the salad oil, beating them
lightly with a small wire whisk and gradually adding half the
light ale. Then beat in the remainder of the ale until the batter
is of the thickness of cream. Add a little more ale if necessary.
The slower and the more lightly you can mix the oil, flour, ale
and egg-yolk the better. Before using it try it with the point of
your finger which dip into the batter; if it readily and smoothly
masks the same it will do. To make the fritters the apples
should not be peeled too soon. Cut each into three or four
slices, then with a cutter take the centre from each and place
them in a plate or in a basin sprinkling the grated rind of a
lemon over them. Dip one piece at a time (meanwhile see that
the deep oil is hot) and then into your hot lard. Fry about 8
pieces at a time and place them on a wire sieve until all are done.
Then coat them with a little hot sugar and salamander them
(put under a hot grill to brown the sugar). Serve them on a
napkin, sugar side upwards, with cream.'

Makes about 40 fritters.

Bananas, slices of pineapple, apricots, peaches etc. can
all be used for fritters.

INCEMEAT

The Palace of Placentia at Greenwich, where Greenwich Hospital now stands, was the birthplace of Henry VIII, Queen Mary I and Queen Elizabeth I. Henry VII kept Christmas at Greenwich Palace in 1486, and the following is an extract from a contemporary recorder.

'*The table at which the King sat was richly decorated and groaned beneath the good fare placed upon it, for there was brawn, roast beef, venison pasty, pheasants, swan, capons, lampreys, pyke in latimer sauce, custard, partridge, fruit, plovers and a huge plum pudding which required the efforts of two men to carry. Afterwards plays were performed and there was much music and dancing, and in the large kitchens after the spit had stopped its ceaseless turning, and the King had dined . . . a merry crowd gathered . . .*

'*. . . and we had, besides a good chine of beef and other good cheer, eighteen mince pies in a dish . . .*'

Samuel Pepys, 6th January 1662.

Mincemeat was originally made with a certain amount of meat in it; nowadays the only ingredient which remains to remind us of this, is the beef suet. It was, of course, a way of preserving meat, so that it could be used throughout the winter in a form other than salting or smoking. This recipe is over 130 years old.

1 lb. (2 cups) (454 gr.) each of:
  stoned and chopped raisins,
  currants, mixed chopped
  candied peel; apples, peeled,
  cored and chopped

grated zest of 3 oranges and
  3 lemons
1 tablespoon mixed nutmeg,
  clove, cinnamon
½ bottle brandy

1 lb. (2 cups) (454 gr.) brown
  sugar
1 lb. (2 cups) (454 gr.) grated
  suet

1 lb. (454 gr.) lean roasted
  sirloin beef, chopped fine*
½ bottle Madeira, port, or
  sweet sherry
*not essential, but traditional

Thoroughly mix the dry ingredients and place in an earthenware or glass pan, and press down level. Pour the brandy and wine on the top. Exclude air as far as possible by closing the pan with a tight-fitting lid, or foil, to limit the evaporation of the spirits. Keep in a cool place for 2 weeks, stir well, and the mincemeat will be ready for use. It will keep indefinitely if well capped. Put into jars if preferred, and pour a little brandy on the top to improve taste and keeping qualities. Makes about 9 lb. (4¼ k.)

TO MAKE MINCEPIES. Roll out either puff, (page 113) or shortcrust pastry (page 109) and cut into small circles to fit patty pans. Fill with mincemeat, then damp the edges and cover with pastry, press down, brush tops with milk or beaten egg, and bake for 15 minutes in a hot oven (400°F.). Serve with Brandy Butter (page 54).

ICED MINCEPIES, a Victorian fancy, are made as above, but without the pastry lid. Instead, after cooking for 10 minutes the tops are covered with egg whites beaten until stiff with sugar. The pies are then returned to a low oven (200°F.) until a pale brown.

Greenwich Market, at the entrance to Turnpin Lane, c. 1900. This market, which now caters mainly for fruit and vegetables, still goes on.

SAUCES

'Dolly's Chop House in St Paul's Churchyard for chops, steaks or a "cut direct" from the joint, with well-boiled mealy potatoes, is particularly good, and this with excellent wine ought to satisfy anybody who, like the young guardsman, could rough it very well on beefsteaks and port . . .' London at Table, *1851. Boswell remarks in his* London Journal: *'A beefsteak-house is a most excellent place to dine at . . . My dinner (beef, bread and beer, and waiter) was only a shilling.' These chop houses also served a meat breakfast, usually steak or a large chop with bread and beer. A favourite way of serving thick mutton chops grilled over charcoal was with pickled walnuts, so beloved by many of Dickens's characters in* Sketches by Boz. *A sauce was made from pickled walnuts for eating with boiled beef; it is also very good with chops, and has the curious name of*

WOW-WOW SAUCE

For serving with stewed or boiled beef, chops, steaks etc. From *The Cook's Oracle* by Dr William Kitchiner, 1817.

4 large pickled walnuts	1 tablespoon chopped parsley
2 oz. ($\frac{1}{4}$ cup) (57 gr.) butter	1 teaspoon made mustard
1 tablespoon flour	$\frac{1}{2}$ pint (1 cup) (0·285 l.) stock
1 tablespoon each of: vinegar, mushroom catchup or Port wine	

Chop the parsley very fine and quarter the walnuts, then dice them and set aside. Melt the butter in a saucepan, stir in the flour, then add the stock (or beef broth the meat was cooked in for boiled beef), stirring well to avoid lumps. When smooth,

Preparing for Queen Victoria's Diamond Jubilee, St Paul's Churchyard, 1897; photographer, Paul Martin.

add the vinegar, catchup or Port and the made mustard. Let it simmer together till it is as thick as you wish it. Put in the parsley and pickled walnuts and serve with the meat. The recipe finishes with: 'If you think the above not sufficiently piquante add to it some capers, or a minced Eschalot [shallot], or one or two teaspoonsful of Essence of Anchovy, or Horseradish vinegar.'

REFORM CLUB SAUCE for chops.

Invented by Alexis Soyer, the famous chef of the Reform Club.

2 tablespoons vinegar	2 tablespoons beet, matchstick thin
2 tablespoons caster (extra fine) sugar	2 gherkins sliced, matchstick thin
1 tablespoon black peppercorns	
1 small finely chopped onion	1 hard-boiled egg-white, sliced very thin
2 slices, matchstick thin, chopped tongue or ham	1 tablespoon redcurrant jelly
$\frac{1}{2}$ pint (1 cup) (0·285 l.) brown gravy or stock	

Put the vinegar, sugar, crushed peppercorns and finely chopped onion in a saucepan and cook over a high flame until the onions are soft. Add the gravy or stock and redcurrant jelly and simmer for a few minutes, then strain. Add the chopped ham or tongue, beet, egg-white and gherkins to the liquid and bring to the boil, then serve hot with the chops.

Makes approximately 2 cups. See also page 69.

5

POTTED CHEESE, PICKLED ONIONS

The Apothecaries' Garden was established in 1673 and frequently visited by the famous Linnaeus. This physic garden, still in existence, was the gift to the Apothecaries Company by Sir Hans Sloane on his death in 1753.

The Old Swan, alas no longer, was famous in Pepys's time as a favourite resort for townsfolk who came to it by land or water. 'All night down by water, a most pleasant passage and come hither by 2 o'clock, and so walked from the Old Swan home and there to bed . . .' 12th July 1665.

In the eighteenth century it was the meeting place for many of the literati: *Smollett in a letter to a friend wrote: 'Messrs Wilton and Russell and all our brotherhood at the Swan.' It was also the goal of the Doggett's Coat and Badge Race, which still continues, and the setting of Tom Tug's song in the Dibden opera* The Waterman.

> *'Then farewell, my trim-built wherry,*
> *Oars and coat and badge farewell,*
> *Never more at Chelsea ferry*
> *Shall your Thomas take a spell.'*

POTTED CHEESE

1 lb. (454 gr.) hard cheese, such as Cheddar or Cheshire
$\frac{1}{4}$ pint ($\frac{1}{2}$ cup) (0·142 l.) sweet sherry or sweet white wine
$\frac{1}{2}$ teaspoon dry mustard powder
$\frac{1}{2}$ teaspoon powdered mace
a pinch cayenne pepper
4 oz. ($\frac{1}{2}$ cup) (114 gr.) butter, plus more butter for pouring
  over the top

Grate the cheese and pound with all the other ingredients very thoroughly, pouring in the wine last and mixing it very well so that the whole is of a creamy consistency (Nowadays this can be done in a blender.) Put into small pots and cover the top with melted butter and when it is set cover with foil and keep in a cool place. It will keep for some time as long as the butter seal is not broken.

PICKLED ONIONS

3 lb. (1$\frac{1}{2}$ kg.) small button onions
1 quart (4 cups) (1·142 l.) white vinegar
1 tablespoon each of cloves, whole allspice, mace
1 teaspoon black peppercorns
4 small chillies
a pinch of cinnamon
1 heaped tablespoon sugar

Bring the spices, sugar and vinegar to boiling point in a covered saucepan and stand for a few hours until the mixture is cool. If a mild spiced vinegar is wanted then strain the vinegar before covering the onions. Peel the onions and pack into wide-mouthed jars, cover with the cold vinegar and seal. Leave for at least a month before using, but they will keep at least a year if the jars are airtight.

The Old Swan, adjacent to the Apothecaries' Garden on the east side, Chelsea, c. 1858.

LONDON BUNS

London Buns are nowadays like fat, long, thick fingers covered with a white icing. This old recipe is richer and makes most delectable spicy, orange-flavoured tea cakes.

2 lb. (8 cups) (907 gr.) flour
4 oz. (½ cup) (114 gr.) sugar
3 oz. (3 heaped tablespoons) (85 gr.) butter
1 oz. (28 gr.) yeast
2 heaped tablespoons chopped candied orange peel
a pinch of nutmeg
1 pint (2 cups) (0·57 l.) milk
1 beaten egg and a little coarse sugar mixed, for glazing

Sift the flour, sugar and nutmeg into a large basin. Melt the butter in a saucepan and add the milk, so that it is just lukewarm. Dissolve the yeast in this, but see that it is tepid otherwise it will kill the yeast. When the yeast mixture has liquefied, pour into the centre of the flour and mix well, then add the finely cut candied peel. Cover and leave to rise in a warm place for about 2 hours or until it is almost double in size. Knead well and make into about 24 round or finger-shaped buns. Put them onto a greased baking sheet and let them double in size before baking in a hot oven (400°F.) for about ½ hour. Five minutes before they are ready brush the tops over with the beaten egg and sugar mixed and put them back in the oven to dry out and glaze.

Makes about 24.

Three Smart Girls, Victoria Park, Bethnal Green, 1898; photographer Paul Martin. Victoria Park occupies over 200 acres, and has a good boating lake. It is the principal park of East London.

9

BUBBLE AND SQUEAK

Many poor children at this time were still 'mudlarks' to keep themselves in food. Mayhew in 1851 had this to say: 'The mudlarks generally live in some court or alley in the neighbourhood of the river, and, as the tide recedes, crowds of boys and little girls, some old men, and many old women . . . scatter themselves along the shore when the tide is sufficiently low . . . and collect whatever they happen to find, such as coals, bits of old-iron, rope, bones, and copper nails that drop from the ships . . . "It is very cold in winter" he said, "to stand in the mud without shoes," but he did not mind it in the summer. He had been three years mudlarking, and supposed he should remain a mudlark all his life. Some days he earned a 1d, and some days 4d; he never earned 8d in one day, that would have been a "jolly lot of money".'

London Labour and the London Poor

BUBBLE AND SQUEAK
*'When 'midst the frying pan, in accents savage,
The beef so surly, quarrels with the cabbage.'* Anon.

The name is onomatopoeic, from the sound it makes when cooking. Originally it was made with slices of cold salt beef, freshly cooked cabbage, fried up in beef dripping, but later on it was made with cold green vegetables (either cabbage or brussels sprouts), chopped onion, and cold potato. The following recipe comes from Cassell's *Dictionary of Cookery*, 1877.

'Dissolve 2 or 3 ounces of beef dripping in a frying pan. Cut some thin slices of cold boiled or roast beef and fry them slightly, a nice brown. Mix some cold greens of any kind with a few mashed potatoes, shred onion, if liked, salt and pepper, and fry, stirring all the time.'

Nowadays it is usually made as follows:

Allow at least 4 cups of cooked green vegetables to the same of mashed potato, adding 1 medium sliced onion, to 8 slices of chopped beef. The vegetables and meat should all be mixed well together and fried on both sides until crispy brown. It is a simple, tasty way of using up the remains of a joint and vegetables, and much improved if served with a good tomato ketchup or a dash of Worcestershire sauce.

Above quantities serve about 4.

Three smart boys, Lambeth, c. 1903; photographer, Paul Martin.

POACHED EGGS

The King's Head is mentioned by John Stow (1525-1605) as 'one of the fair inns of Southwark'. Before the Reformation it was known as 'The Pope's Head' but this building was burnt down in the great fire of Southwark in 1676, but by the early eighteenth century it had been rebuilt retaining the seventeenth century galleries and 'enjoying a good trade'. The inn of the photograph was again rebuilt in 1879. Two other famous inns were nearby: the Tabard of which Chaucer wrote, 'Byfel that in that seasoun a day, In Southwerk at the Tabard as I lay . . .' was demolished about 1876 but a modern pub now exists on the site. The George, formerly the St George and the Dragon, alone remains today together with its yard, more or less, intact. Dickens referred to it in Little Dorrit as the place where Tip goes to write his begging letters to Clennam. The first reference to The George was in 1554.

' . . . and there staid at the King's Head, and eat a breakfast of eggs . . . '

Samuel Pepys, 18th August 1662

EGGS POACHED WITH A SAUCE OF MINCED HAM
Adapted from *The Cook's Oracle* by Dr Kitchiner, 1817.

8 eggs
boiling water seasoned with a little salt and a dash of lemon
  juice or vinegar
8 slices toast or fried bread

Yard of the King's Head Inn, Borough High Street, c. 1870.

FOR THE SAUCE
8 slices boiled ham, minced
1 pint (2 cups) (0.57 l.) stock
1 small grated onion
4 pickled gherkins or 1 small pickled cucumber, finely chopped
1 tablespoon chopped parsley with 1 teaspoon *beurre manié*
  (a nut of butter rolled in flour)
juice of either $\frac{1}{2}$ orange or lemon

First make the sauce by boiling up all the sauce ingredients except the *beurre manié* and the orange or lemon juice. Let it simmer for about 15 minutes, then stir in the *beurre manié* to thicken it slightly. Keep it warm whilst you are poaching the eggs. Bring the seasoned water to the boil and then break an egg into a cup and slip it into the boiling water very gently, and simmer until the white is just set, then remove with a skimmer on to a warmed dish and keep warm. When all the eggs are cooked, squeeze over the orange or lemon juice and pour the sauce over them. Arrange the slices of toast cut in half around the edges.   Serves 4.

Another nineteenth-century sauce for poached eggs was:

BURNT BUTTER
Heat up 2 oz. ($\frac{1}{4}$ cup) (57 gr.) of butter in a saucepan until it is a light brown colour, then add $1\frac{1}{2}$ tablespoons vinegar, 1 tablespoon capers, salt and pepper. Let it heat up and get a medium dark brown. This is enough for 4 eggs.

BOODLE'S ORANGE FOOL AND FRUIT CAKE

Boodle's was founded in 1763 and was originally called the Savoir Faire. The club building was erected in 1765. One of its earliest members was Edward Gibbon, the author of The History of the Decline and Fall of the Roman Empire *and other books. Several of his letters, dated in the 1770s, were written from the club. See also pages 61, 93 for further information about London Clubs.*

BOODLE'S ORANGE FOOL

From Boodle's Club, *c.* 1920. This simple dish is truly delicious.

4 large oranges
2 lemons
1 pint (2 cups) (0·57 l.) cream
6 sponge cakes about 4 in. × 2 in.
2 tablespoons sugar, approx.

Finely grate the rind of 1 lemon and 2 oranges, then squeeze the juice from all the fruit and sweeten to taste and mix together (the above quantity of sugar might not be sweet enough, depending on the quality of the oranges). Cut the sponge cakes into 4 pieces each and put into the bottom of the dish they will be served from. Pour the cream into the fruit juice and rind, stirring very lightly. Pour this mixture over the cakes, and leave for at least 2 hours (it can stay for 4 hours) to let the juice and cream penetrate the sponge cakes.

Serves 4-6.

BOODLE'S FRUIT CAKE

1 lb. (4 cups) (454 gr.) flour	1 lb. (2 cups) (454 gr.)
8 oz. (1 cup) (227 gr.) butter	seedless raisins
8 oz. (1 cup) (227 gr.) sugar	2 teaspoons bicarbonate soda
½ pint (1 cup) (0·285 l.) milk	2 eggs

Sift the flour and bicarbonate of soda together, then rub in the butter. Then mix in the raisins and the sugar. Beat the eggs with three-quarters of the milk and beat in for 5 minutes. If it seems too stiff then add the remainder of the milk, and beat well. Grease and line an 8-inch cake tin (or use a non-stick tin), and preheat the oven to 325°F. Cover the top with greased paper, and bake for 1 hour, then lower the heat to 300°F. and continue baking without the paper for a further 3½ hours. Leave to cool in the tin, then put on to a wire rack to get cold.

Serves about 10.

BOILED SALT BEEF, CARROTS AND DUMPLINGS WITH PARSLEY SAUCE

At the beginning of this century Hampstead could be reached only by stage coaches, which ran twice a day from different parts of London. Once or twice a year the Cockneys from East London made this trip with their families, and enjoyed the tea gardens, the inns, the fun of the fair on the Heath, and most of all perhaps the fresh air and open spaces which they and their children so sadly needed. In many cases the August Bank Holiday and Christmas Day were the only days in the year when they were free from work.

> 'It is a goodly sight through the clear air,
> From Hampstead's healthy height to see at once,
> England's vast Capital in fair expanse . . . '
>
> *James Beattie.*

Pease Pudding (page 30) is often served as well with this dish.

4 lb. (1·816 kg.) salted brisket or silverside beef	2 lb. (907 gr.) carrots
	1 head celery
2 large onions stuck with cloves	2 leeks
	sprig of thyme and parsley
1 teaspoon mustard powder	pepper

FOR THE SAUCE

2 tablespoons chopped parsley	2 tablespoons flour
1 tablespoon butter	1 pint (2 cups) (0·57 l.) stock

Put the beef in a large saucepan with the herbs, mustard, whole onions and pepper, then barely cover with water, bring to the boil and simmer gently for 30 minutes to the pound. After 1 hour add all the other vegetables, sliced according to taste.

The vegetables are served with the meat, and if not serving pease pudding (which is boiled in a cloth with the meat, [see page 30] a sauce is made by melting the butter, stirring in the flour, then adding 1 pint of the stock and 2 tablespoons chopped parsley, it all being well stirred to avoid lumps. Transfer to a sauce boat, keep warm and serve separately.

DUMPLINGS

8 oz. (2 cups) (227 gr.) self-raising flour	4 oz. (1 cup) (114 gr.) grated suet
2 tablespoons grated horseradish*	¼ pint (½ cup) (0·142 l.) water
salt and pepper	

*chopped herbs can be substituted for the horseradish, if preferred

Make the dumplings ½ hour before the meat is cooked. Mix the flour, salt and pepper, and suet together, then add enough cold water to make a stiff paste. Put on to a floured board and shape into little balls about the size of a large walnut, for they will swell up a lot in cooking. Poke a small hole in the top and put in either the horseradish or herbs, and squeeze tightly to secure. When the meat and vegetables are cooked, remove to a warm dish and keep warm, then poach the dumplings, about four at a time in the simmering stock, with the lid on, for about 10 minutes. They will float to the top when ready. Drain, and serve around the beef together with the vegetables.

Makes about 16 dumplings.

Bank Holiday crowd on Hampstead Heath, 1902.

TOAD-IN-THE-HOLE

The name Aldwych comes from eald, *old, and* wic, *town or settlement and it is said that when King Alfred conquered London from the Danes he allotted this territory to them, for their occupation outside the city. It formerly contained quite a large number of theatres of which only three remain; the Aldwych, the Duchess and the Strand. The Gaiety Theatre was built early in the nineteenth century, and as its name implies was used mostly for extremely successful musical comedies: it is now demolished. Nearby was the famous Lyceum Theatre, built in 1765 and then called the Lyceum Great Room. It was at that time a picture gallery, but in 1794 Dr Arnold the composer rebuilt the back part, and converted it into a small theatre which was the scene of many diverse entertainments, from Dibdin's* Entertainment Sans Souci *to Philip Astley's remarkable circus of horses and the world-famous clowns, Grimaldi, Johannot, Dubois, Laurent and Wallack. In the nineteenth century it was the home of Sir Henry Irving and his company, and from then on became well-known for melodrama and spectacle of the highest order.*

Toad-in-the-hole has now become a dull dish, but in the nineteenth and early twentieth centuries it was a dish well worth making. I have only seen it made with sausages in the batter, but Soyer has a recipe for using up jugged hare with redcurrant jelly which sounds excellent. I have made it with chopped ham steaks, liberally covered with made mustard and a trickle of honey, also with lamb chops; trimmings from rump or fillet steak, including a kidney. The following recipe is dated 1853.

6 trimmed neck of lamb chops without bone	1 teaspoon chopped mint
	2 eggs
2 lamb's kidneys	6 oz. (1½ cups) (170 gr.) flour
1 medium onion finely grated	½ pint (1 cup) (0·285 l.) milk
1 medium sized cucumber or 6 mushrooms	4 tablespoons light beer
	salt and pepper

First make the batter by beating the eggs, and then mixing together the flour and a pinch of salt and pepper. Add the eggs, beating well, then add the beer, and finally the milk, beating well until free from lumps. Leave to stand to get the air in. Then peel and slice the cucumber, or mushrooms if using, and lightly salt them. Trim the chops and kidneys and grill them for about a minute on each side, just to brown them and seal the juices. Put the meat, drained cucumber or mushrooms, grated onion, and chopped mint into a deep ovenproof dish and sprinkle with a little pepper. Give a final beat to the batter, then pour over the contents of the dish. Put, uncovered, into a pre-heated oven (375°F.) for about 1 hour, or until the batter has risen and is a nice golden-brown colour.

Serves 6.

Time for a chat outside the Gaiety Theatre, Aldwych, 1913.

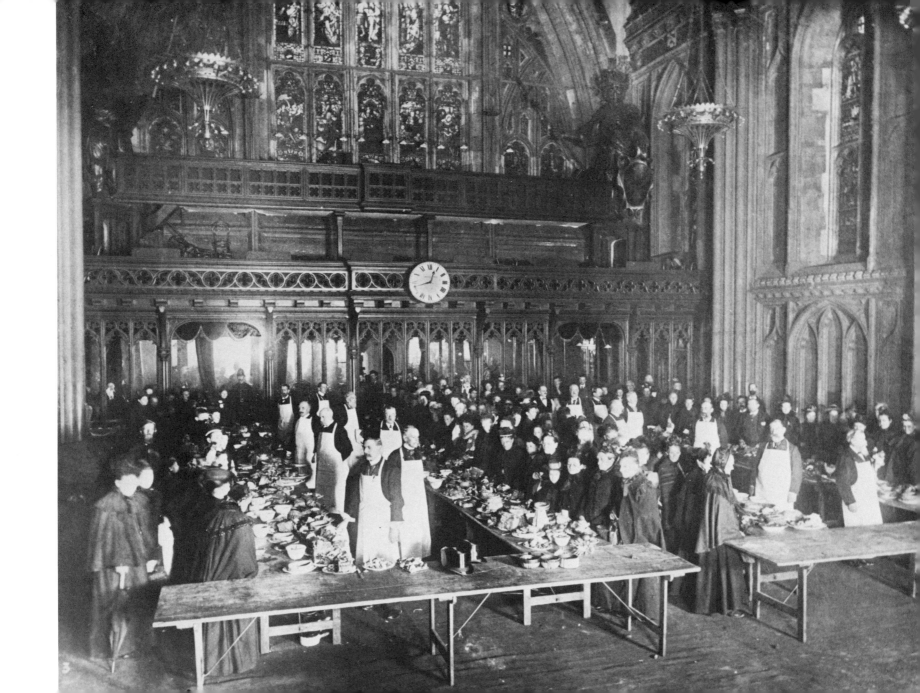

LORD MAYOR'S TRIFLE

The first Mayor of London was Henry FitzEylwin about 1191, but he was not referred to as 'Lord Mayor', the earliest reference to this title being 1283. On 9th November each year there is a pageant held in London called the 'Lord Mayor's Show' which terminates in a banquet. The Mansion House, which is the official residence of the Lord Mayor, has a magnificent dining-room called the Egyptian Hall. Traditionally turtle soup enriched with Madeira wine was served, followed by either a roasted baron of beef or venison. Alderman's Walk is the name given in the City of London to the longest and best cut of meat sliced from a haunch of venison or mutton.

LORD MAYOR'S TRIFLE

Adapted from Cassell's *Dictionary of Cookery*, 1877.

Well-made trifle can take its place with some of the fine old sweet dishes, but, alas, nowadays it is often made with jelly and package custard powder.

6 sponge cakes (about 4 in. × 2 in.)
24 small ratafia or almond biscuits, about an inch across
6 tablespoons strawberry or raspberry jam
½ pint (1 cup) (0·285 l.) cream
8 macaroons
¼ pint (½ cup) (0·142 l.) brandy, or brandy and sherry mixed
1 pint (2 cups) (0·57 l.) custard (see below)
chopped nuts and glacé fruit to decorate

TO MAKE THE CUSTARD
1 pint (2 cups) (0·57 l.) milk
2 tablespoons caster sugar or vanilla sugar if liked
4 egg-yolks well beaten

Beat the egg-yolks well. Boil the milk slowly with the sugar until it has dissolved. Pour the sweetened milk over the eggs, stir well, and return to the pan. Stir over moderate heat (or preferably in a double boiler) until the liquid will coat the back of the spoon. If it is allowed to boil it will curdle. (This can be avoided to a certain extent by adding a teaspoon of cornflour [cornstarch] to the milk before starting.) Remove from the heat and stir to prevent a skin forming. (Brandy or lemon or cinnamon or chocolate can all be added as flavouring if the custard is to be poured into small pots as a dish on its own.)

Slice the sponge cakes and put on the bottom of a deep dish, then add the macaroons, crumbled up, and the small ratafias and pour over the brandy. Leave to soak up, then spread the jam over, then the cold custard. About ½ hour before serving add the well whipped cream piled high over the top and decorate with chopped nuts and chopped glacé fruit.

Serves 8.

Distributing food to poor widows the day after the Lord Mayor's Banquet, at Guildhall, 1897.

FISH PIE

A vast amount of London's prosperity has been due to its being situated on the Thames, which formerly was much more used than it is today. John Norden writing in 1594 estimated that 40,000 people were maintained by the river alone. About 150 years ago it contained many fine fish, such as salmon, flounders, smelts, barbel, eels, roach, dace, lamprey, not forgetting the large amounts of whitebait that were caught annually at Greenwich, Woolwich, Blackwall and Gravesend, see page 47. By the 1840s fish were becoming scarce, and today they are negligible. The name is thought to come from the Latin Thamesis, *meaning the broad water.*

'Sweet Thames, run softly, till I end my Song'
Edmund Spenser, Prothalamion.

FISH PIE

2 lb. (approx. 1 kg.) filleted white fish or smoked haddock or cod*

1 pint (2 cups) (0·57 l.) milk

¼ teaspoon fennel or dill seeds

cayenne pepper, salt

1 heaped tablespoon cornflour (cornstarch)

1 small grated onion, shallot, or garlic

1 lb. (454 gr.) peeled tomatoes, fresh or canned

2 tablespoons grated cheese

4 cups mashed potato

1 tablespoon chopped parsley

*smoked fish gives a very definite flavour, so long as it is not too salty. A mixture of smoked and fresh fish is good, and if available chunks of shellfish, such as scallops, prawns or lobster make an excellent fish pie. The better the fish, the better the pie.

First put the fish skin-side up under a hot grill for a few minutes, so as to be able to remove the skin easily, and make certain it is quite free from bones. Put into a large shallow pan, cover with the milk, add the fennel seeds and pepper, bring to the boil and poach very lightly on both sides for about 10 minutes. Remove the fish to an ovenproof casserole, cream the cornflour with a little water, and stir into the hot milk, stirring all the time so that it is smooth. Add the tomatoes (drained if canned), the cheese, onion, and parsley and when they are all well mixed taste for seasoning. Pour over the fish and mix well. The sauce should be on the thin side for it will thicken in cooking. Meanwhile mash the potatoes well and layer over the top making sure that you start around the edges, pressing it down, so that the sauce doesn't push through. Put into a moderate oven, 350°F., and bake for about ½ hour or until the top is gently browned. This pie can be made ahead of time and heated in the oven, but allow longer time for browning the top.

Serves 4.

If any of the pie is left over, mix the fish, sauce and potato together, add a beaten egg and enough flour so that the mixture holds its shape. Make into small round cakes, roll in more flour, or breadcrumbs, and fry until golden on both sides in shallow oil. Smoked haddock makes excellent fishcakes, and the ratio should be about half fish and half potato.

'. . . the fruitful Thame', c. 1870; photographer, James Hedderley.

JAM ROLY-POLY

The royal coat of arms shown on the wall of the inn in the photograph was given by Queen Victoria, in recognition of the landlord's bravery. In 1837 the Queen was being driven with her mother, the Duchess of Kent, in a carriage without a drag chain. The horses became restive and plunged violently. A bad accident was only avoided by the promptness of Mr Turner, the landlord of the Fox and Crown, who grabbed at the reins. The Queen and her mother rested for a while in the house. The coat of arms, which is now in the Highate Literary and Scientific Institution in South Grove, bears the inscription: '6th July 1837. This coat of arms is a grant from Queen Victoria for services rendered to Her Majesty while in danger travelling down this hill.' At the time of the incident the inn was called the 'Fox under the Hill' Tavern.

Highgate cemetery holds the remains of many famous people: Charles Dickens's parents, his wife, his child Dora, and many other relatives lie there; also George Eliot, Karl Marx and William Friese-Greene, the early English cinematographer.

Highgate is over 400 feet above sea-level and has been thought for centuries to be very healthy. 'Upon this hills is most pleasant dwelling, yet not so pleasant as healthful; for the expert inhabitants there report that divers that have beene long visited with sickness, not curable by physicke, have in short time repayred their health by that sweet salutarie aire'. John Norden, 1593

JAM ROLY-POLY

This can also be made with golden or corn syrup and is then called Syrup Roll. If the jam or syrup is omitted and sultanas, raisins or currants are added to the dough, it is known as 'Spotted Dick'. This recipe was kindly given to me by Mr R. Smythe of Simpson's-in-the-Strand where it is a regular item on the menu, and has been so for almost a century.

1 lb. (4 cups) (454 gr.) flour	½ pint (1 cup) (0·285 l.)
1 oz. (2 tablespoons) (28 gr.) baking powder	water approx.
	6 oz. (1½ cups) (170 gr.)
½ lb. (227 gr.) jam, preferably	grated suet
raspberry, strawberry or	2 oz. (¼ cup) (57 gr.) sugar
apricot, slightly warmed	a pinch of salt

Sieve together the flour, salt and baking powder. Mix in the sugar and the grated or finely chopped suet. Mix with the cold water, adding it gradually until it makes a firm paste. (You might find that just under the ½ pint is enough.) Put out on to a floured board and roll out to a square of about 14 inches. Spread with the slightly warmed jam to within 1 inch of the edges. Fold over two of the sides to meet in the middle: then moisten the back edge and roll up from front to back. Lay in buttered greaseproof paper, roll up, and tie securely. Put into a steamer over boiling water, or wrap in a cloth and boil in boiling water for 1½ hours. If a cloth is used it should be wrung out in boiling water and sprinkled with flour on the inside before rolling up the pudding. Serve with a sauce-boat of warmed jam.

Enough for 6-8.

This roly-poly can also be baked like pastry on a greased baking tin in a hot oven (400°F.) for about 40 minutes. In this case sprinkle the jam with breadcrumbs before rolling up.

CRUMPETS

'Mama, why mayn't I, when I dine,
Eat ham, and goose, and drink port wine?
And why mayn't I, as well as you,
Eat pudding, soup, and mutton, too?
Because, my child, it is not right,
To spoil the youthful appetite.'

Mrs Turner, *Cautionary Tales*

This little jingle expresses perfectly the Victorian and Edwardian attitude to children's food. Nevertheless, crumpets are a delicious tea-time treat for all ages. The London variety have small air-holes on the top, and when toasted, the butter seeps through in a most succulent way. They are extremely good for a high tea or a light meal with poached eggs on top.

1 lb. (4 cups) (454 gr.) plain flour	1 heaped teaspoon dried yeast
1 teaspoon salt	2 teaspoons warm water
1 teaspoon sugar	$\frac{1}{4}$ teaspoon bicarbonate of soda
1 pint (2 cups) (0·57 l.) warm milk	

Sift the flour into a basin and add the salt. Heat the milk until tepid then dissolve the sugar in half of it, and sprinkle the yeast on top. (Do not make the milk too warm for you will kill the yeast.) Leave for 10 minutes or until it froths up, then add to the centre of the flour with the rest of the warm milk and beat very well for 5 or 10 minutes. Cover and leave to rise in a warm place. Dissolve the bicarbonate of soda in the warm water and add to the risen dough, then leave, covered, to rise again. If you have 3-4-inch plain rings, then lightly grease them, also a griddle, or a heavy frying pan, and heat them up as you would for pancakes or drop scones. Put the rings, if using them, on to the hot griddle or pan, and drop tablespoonfuls of the mixture into them or into the pan. Let it cook until the top is set and full of holes, and the bottom a pale biscuit colour. Remove the rings, if using, turn the crumpets over and let them dry out for 2 minutes on the other side. Regulate the heat, especially if using electricity, so that the griddle does not become too hot and burn. Remove the crumpets with a cloth, and let them cool on a rack. When serving, toast them lightly on both sides and serve with butter on the top side (with the holes).

Makes about 12.

EGGS BENEDICT are an excellent American invention. They consist of toasted crumpets or muffins (page 40) with a slice of grilled ham the same size on top, then a poached egg, all covered with Hollandaise sauce, or English Butter Sauce, page 75.

Beside the Long Water, Kensington Gardens, c. 1889.

MIXED GRILL WITH DEVILLED BUTTER

The first Thames Tunnel was constructed by the Brunels and opened in 1843 for pedestrians, It was bought by the East London Railway Co., and converted for railway use in 1866. However, the first London Underground railway (The Metropolitan Railway Co.) opened from Paddington to Farringdon in 1863, using steam traction. The first section of the (steam) District Railway opened from High Street, Kensington to Gloucester Road in 1868, and the first Tube Railway in the world with cable-operated cars ran from Tower Bridge to the Surrey side of the Thames in 1869. In 1884 the Metropolitan and District Railways extended to form the 'Inner Circle'. It was worked by both companies, and operated by steam. It was in 1890 that the first Electric Tube Railway (City and South London Co.) in London, ran from King William Street, E.C.4, to Stockwell. Small electric locomotives were used and the carriages had no windows. The 'Inner Circle' was electrified in 1905.

MIXED GRILL WITH DEVILLED BUTTER

Ideally should be cooked over charcoal. A good mixed grill should have the following ingredients: an inch-thick chop of centre-loin lamb or mutton; a lamb's kidney or a thick piece of lambs' or calves' liver; several rashers of bacon, 1 or 2 sausages, a grilled tomato and a healthy portion of grilled mushrooms. The grill should be pre-heated until it is very hot, the chop should be trimmed of surplus fat, the fatty edges nicked with a pair of scissors to prevent it curling up, and the whole chop beaten for a minute to make it tender and prevent shrinking. Start by grilling the chop, for it will take the longest (about 10-15 minutes depending on thickness), then about 5 minutes after it has been cooking, add the kidney, then the liver brushed with oil, the tomatoes and bacon. When half cooked, season with salt and pepper. Turn them, as one side becomes cooked and brown, and do not overcook. Put the mushrooms under the rack so that they cook in the juices and when all are ready, put the grill on top of the heat, remove the cooked meats to a warmed dish or plate, and let the mushrooms finish cooking on top, turning them at least once. While it is cooking, make the devilled butter by mixing 2 pats of butter per person with a few drops of Worcestershire sauce, cayenne pepper, salt, and freshly ground black pepper, and put 1 pat on the chop and 1 on the kidney. Garnish with parsley or watercress and serve with fried potatoes.

Serves 1.

See also Devilled Kidneys, page 57.

'Inner Circle' Metropolitan and District Railway, Charing Cross Station, 1894.

PEASE PUDDING

'. . . there are many others vending papers in the public thorough-fares, who are mere traders resorting to no other acts for the disposal of their goods than a simple cry or exposition of them ; and many of these are but poor, humble, struggling, and inoffensive dealers.'
Henry Mayhew, London Labour and the London Poor, *1851.*

'Pease-porridge hot, pease-porridge cold,
Pease-porridge in the pot, nine days old.'
Newest Christmas Box, c. 1797.

By the nineteenth century it was known as 'pease pudding' and was sold hot by street traders, from a heavy tin pot wrapped around with a thick cloth to retain the heat. Hot, young green peas boiled in the pods were also sold, the criers calling 'Hot peas-cod'. These whole pease were dipped in melted butter with a little pepper, salt and vinegar, then drawn through the teeth to extract the peas. The condiments and butter were supplied by the vendor; basins and spoons were also provided.

PEASE PUDDING is a purée of dried split peas: it is extremely good served with hot boiled salted or pickled pork, salted or corned beef (see page 16), ham or sausages. It is also now available in cans.

1 lb. (2 cups) (454 gr.) yellow split peas (the green variety
  can also be used but it is not traditional) soaked overnight
1 large sliced onion
1 large diced rasher of bacon, or a hambone
1 tablespoon butter
1 teaspoon Worcestershire sauce
salt and pepper
water or stock to over 2 inches above the top of the peas*

*In the old days the peas were put into a floured pudding cloth
  and boiled with the pork or beef, but few people have sauce-
  pans large enough today to hold all the ingredients.

Strain the water from the soaked split peas then put into a large saucepan with the onion and the diced bacon, salt, pepper and enough water or stock to come to at least 2 inches above the top of the peas. Cover, and bring to the boil, then simmer for about 2 hours, or until the peas are a purée and almost all the liquid has been absorbed. Stir from time to time to prevent sticking. When ready, taste for seasoning, add the Worcester-shire sauce and then beat in the butter. When cold it will thicken up a lot, so for reheating add a little more liquid and stir well. This purée can also be made into an excellent soup, by thinning it down with more stock, milk or a mixture of both. It can be most successfully pressure cooked, the time being 30 minutes after pressure is reached with the water 1 inch above the peas.
Serves 6.

The Magazine Seller, Ludgate Circus, c. 1900 ; photographer, Paul Martin.

VOTES FOR WOMEN

Emmeline Pankhurst was born in Manchester in 1858, the daughter of Robert Goulden, a calico-printer. She married in 1879 and her husband, a barrister, was also an advocate of women's suffrage, and she served with him on the committee which promoted the Married Women's Property Act. She helped to found the Women's Franchise League in 1889 and took part in many meetings and demonstrations, mostly in London. She left the Liberal Party when they failed to make votes for women part of their programme, and was instrumental in founding the non-party Women's Social and Political Union. She spent some time in prison for upholding her views and by 1903 had been joined by her eldest daughter Christabel. Both went on hunger-strikes in prison and were released on the grounds of ill-health.

At the beginning of the 1914-18 War, Mrs and Miss Pankhurst lent their organization to the cause of national service, and in 1918 they saw the victory of their ultimate goal, the passing of the Representation of the People Act which included suffrage for women. At the time of her death in 1928 she was the Conservative candidate for Whitechapel and St George's, having joined that party when the bill was passed. I feel that Mrs Pankhurst is her own recipe for bravery, indomitable spirit, and courage.

'Women's Lib', 1912. Mrs Pankhurst addressing a crowd in Trafalgar Square.

ACARONI CHEESE

In many ways the numerous exhibitions which were held in London from the time of the Great Exhibition of 1851 were successors to the Pleasure Gardens (see page 51), for they offered similar attractions in a more ordered, restrained and formal manner. There was always the 'great attraction': 'Venice by Night' at Earl's Court, with waterways, gondolas and palazzos. In 1908 at the White City, there was a huge revolving chair-a-plane called a 'Flip-Flap'. Food, drink and spectacle were the ingredients, and the public loved it. Many foreign dishes were given an English slant, and some became regular, popular items of the daily menu. Rich, gadabout young men were termed 'macaronis' in the nineteenth century.

MACARONI CHEESE can be a really excellent dish when made the following way.

½ lb. (1½ cups) (227 gr.)
  macaroni, the thickest you
  can find
1 pint (2 cups) (0·57 l.) milk
black pepper and a pinch
  of cayenne
½ teaspoon dry mustard
  powder
1 tablespoon butter
1 egg
¾ lb. (3 cups) (340 gr.)
  grated hard Cheddar or
  similar cheese

Cook the macaroni for 20 minutes in boiling salted water: break it up if it is the long, thin variety. Drain well and put back in the saucepan, on a very low heat, with the butter and the milk. Let the macaroni absorb the milk. Then add the peppers and the dry mustard, and mix well each time. Then add the cheese (except 2 tablespoons), remove from the heat and beat until it is all creamy. Finally add the well-beaten egg, pour into a greased ovenproof dish, sprinkle the remaining cheese on top and bake in a quick oven (400°F.) for not longer than 10-15 minutes, just enough to let it set. If it has not browned in this time, do not leave it in the oven for it will dry up, but put it under a hot grill.

The sauce will be curdy and creamy if it is not cooked too much. A few drops of tabasco can be served with it, or more made mustard, or a fresh tomato sauce (see page 63) heated up. This macaroni cheese can be made in advance and heated in a moderate oven (350°F.) (with a little extra cheese sprinkled over the top) for about 25 minutes.

Serves 2 or 4, depending on whether it is a main course or a savoury.

'Venice by Night', at the Earl's Court Exhibition, 1904.

CHOLENT, LATKES

Aldgate was one of the original gates of London and the dwelling house above the gate was occupied by Chaucer from 1374 to 1385. Aldgate and the surrounding neighbourhood have for many years been the centre of a large Jewish community, which is evident today in excellent Jewish restaurants, such as Bloom's by Aldgate East tube station. Cholent, the dish eaten on the Jewish Sabbath when no cooking is permitted, has found its way into the English cuisine in the form of haricot beef or mutton stew.

CHOLENT

8 oz. (1½ cups) (227 gr.) haricot (Lima) beans soaked overnight in cold water to cover	boiling water to cover
	2 tablespoons oil or chicken fat
3 coarsely chopped medium onions	½ teaspoon each: salt, pepper, ginger
8 medium potatoes	1 heaped tablespoon paprika
2 lb. (1 kg.) beef, brisket, short rib or chuck	4 oz. (⅔ cup) (113 gr.) pearl barley*

*In some recipes a large dumpling is used instead of pearl barley. (See page 16).

First sauté the onions in the hot oil or fat until a light brown, then drain them and arrange all ingredients in a large deep casserole in this order: the drained, soaked beans, onions, half the quantity of potatoes, meat (in the middle) surrounded by the pearl barley, then the rest of the potatoes. Season each layer with the spices, then cover with boiling water, or when pearl barley is used to 1 inch above the level of ingredients. Cover with foil, and a lid and cook in the centre of a moderate oven (375°F.) until boiling point is reached. Then lower the heat to 150°F. for about 3-4 hours. In Jewish homes this is either left in a very cool oven or on an asbestos mat over the lowest flame, which will burn with safety overnight. Serves 6-8. Haricot mutton is made the same way, using shoulder or leg of lamb or mutton, usually boned and chopped, omitting the pearl barley and adding 6 medium chopped carrots.

LATKES

Another popular Jewish dish, served with roast veal or on their own.

5 medium potatoes	2 eggs
2 tablespoons self-raising flour	4 tablespoons oil
salt and pepper	

Peel the potatoes, and soak them in cold water for 1 hour. Pat them dry, then grate them and leave to drain. Mix the beaten eggs, flour and seasonings together, then add the potatoes and mix well. Heat the oil, and drop in tablespoonsful of the potato batter, 2 or 3 at a time depending on the size of the pan. When brown on one side turn over and cook the other. It is as well not to have too much heat under the latkes, for the potato must have time to cook through. Drain and serve. If using without meat they can be served with apple sauce, jam, cinnamon, or sour cream. Makes about 24.

Street Market, Aldgate High Street, 1899.

EEF OLIVES

A 'Tower of London' is thought to have been built by the Romans. Shakespeare in Richard II *refers to 'Julius Caesar's ill erected tower', but it is not substantiated, although parts of the Roman wall were incorporated in the defences in Norman times. Six notable prisoners were executed on this place, five of them women: Anne Boleyn; the Countess of Salisbury (aged 71); Jane, Viscountess Rochford, friend of Katherine Howard who was executed at the same time; and Lady Jane Grey. The sixth was the Earl of Essex, the one-time favourite of Queen Elizabeth I. Most executions took place on Tower Hill. Beefeaters are the Yeomen of the Guard in the Royal Household, appointed in 1485 by Henry VII to form part of the royal train at banquets and other occasions. The origin of the word is obscure, but one theory is that it comes from the Anglo-French word* buffeters, *an attendant on the royal buffet.*

BEEF OLIVES
A favourite eighteenth and nineteenth century dish.

12 slices of raw lean beef, rump or sirloin	2 oz. ($1\frac{1}{4}$ cups) (57 gr.) breadcrumbs
grated rind of 1 lemon	1 medium grated onion
2 egg-yolks	1 tablespoon mixed chopped herbs
1 tablespoon cooking oil or fat	pinch of grated nutmeg
2 teaspoons tomato purée or mushroom ketchup	1 pint (2 cups) (0·57 l.) stock
	2 tablespoons flour
	salt and pepper

Flatten the beef slices, which should be about $\frac{1}{2}$ inch thick, about 6 inches long and 5 inches wide, by banging them with a rolling pin. Combine the breadcrumbs, grated onion, lemon rind, herbs, egg-yolks and seasonings and mix well. Put a little on each piece of beef, roll them and secure with a cocktail stick, twine or small skewers. Brown them on all sides in the heated oil, and then sprinkle over the flour. Transfer to an ovenproof dish, add the stock, mushroom ketchup or tomato purée, cover and cook in a moderate oven (350°F.) for $1\frac{1}{2}$ hours. Serve with the vegetables of your choice. These little 'olives' can also be made with rashers of ham, thin slices of pork, veal or salt beef. The fillings can vary to taste, using such foods as lightly fried onions mixed with sausagemeat for veal, and a mixture of chopped rosemary, lemon peel and breadcrumbs with a pinch of mace, for pork.

Serves 4-6.

Beefeater pointing out the Place of Execution at the Tower of London, c. 1895.

MUFFINS, MUFFIN PUDDING

Henry Mayhew, writing in 1851, states that the muffin and crumpet sellers rank among the oldest street traders. They were still to be seen and heard ringing their bell in the streets of London until the 1930s, but alas are now no more. 'A sharp lad of fourteen . . . gave me the following account: I turns out with muffins and crumpets, sir, in October, and continues until it get well into the Spring, according to the weather. I carries a fust-rate article; werry much so . . . If I sells three dozen muffins at ½d. each, and twice that in crumpets, it's a werry fair day, werry fair; all beyond that is a *good* day . . . Perhaps I clears 4s. a week . . . If I has a hextra day's sale, mother'll give me 3d. to go to the play, and that hencourages a young man, you know, sir . . . My best customers is genteel houses, 'cause I sells a genteel thing. I like wet days best, 'cause there's werry respectable ladies what don't keep a servant, and they buys to save themselves going out. We're a great conwenience to the ladies . . . to them as likes a slap-up tea. I can read, but wish I could read easier.'

London Labour and the London Poor.

1 lb. (4 cups) (454 gr.) plain flour	1 teaspoon salt
2 teaspoons sugar	2 teaspoons dried yeast
scant ½ pint (1 cup) (0·285 l.) warm milk	1 egg
	1 oz. (2 tablespoons) (28 gr.) butter, melted

Mix the salt and sifted flour together, then dissolve the sugar in the warm milk and sprinkle the dried yeast over. Leave for about 10 minutes or until it froths up, then add to the flour. Add also the beaten egg and the melted butter and mix to a soft dough. Turn on to a lightly floured board and knead well for 10 minutes, then put into a lightly oiled polythene bag, tie loosely and leave in a warm place to rise until double the size. Turn dough on to the floured board and flatten with the knuckles to remove the air bubbles. Roll out to ½-inch thickness and cut into rounds about 3-3½ inches. Put on to a well-floured board and dust tops with flour. Cover with oiled polythene and leave to rise until double the size. Lightly grease a hot griddle or thick frying pan, and cook the muffins 2 or 3 at a time for about 8 minutes on each side. Serve warm, split, and spread with butter.

Makes about 8.

MUFFIN PUDDING

3 muffins	2 egg-whites, stiffly beaten
3 tablespoons honey	2 heaped tablespoons flour
a pinch of grated nutmeg	¼ pint (½ cup) (0·142 l.) milk
a little butter or margarine	

Butter a 3-pint (2-l.) mould and split the muffins, then pack them into the mould, trickling the honey in between them and sprinkling over the nutmeg. Mix the flour with the milk, add the egg-whites, beaten to a snow, beat until it is like a batter, and pour this over the muffins. Cover with foil and steam over boiling water for 1 hour. Turn out on to a warmed plate and serve with warmed honey.

Serves 4-6. *See also* Eggs Benedict, page 27.

The Muffin Man, c. *1900.*

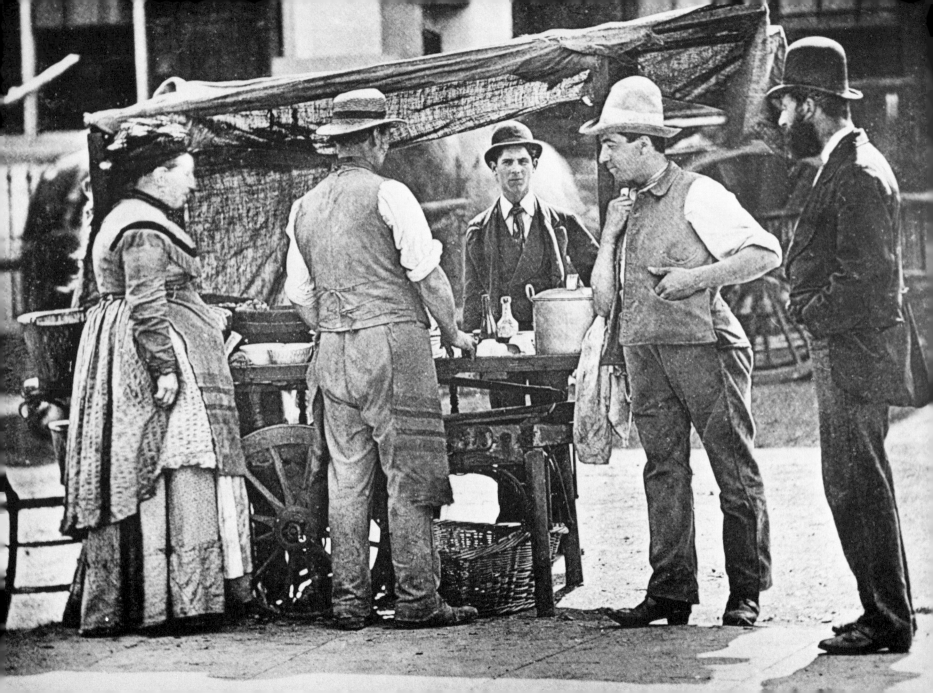

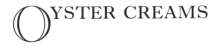

OYSTER CREAMS

'Oysters, whelks and liquor go together invariable; consequence where there's fewest stalls and most publics is the choicest spot for a pitch . . . Hoysters wants no cooking, but whelks, eels, and herrings should be kept in stock cooked to a turn.' The owner of the barrow in the photograph (back to camera) recounted his experiences to the photographer: ' . . . It don't pay more than a poor living, although me and the missus are at this corner with the barrow in all weathers, specially the missus, as I take odd jobs beating carpets etc . . . So the old gal has the most of the weather to herself. I have to start every morning about five for Billingsgate . . . the oysters on the barrow, with pepper, salt and vinegar fetch from a penny to three halfpence . . . I laid in twenty fine herrings this morning. There they are, cooked or soused, as they call it . . . The eel wants good cooking and making into a kind of soup . . . the fish must be cut up, cleaned and dressed, and after that's done boiled in flour and water. The soup has then to be made tasty with spices, parsley, vinegar and pepper. You see that youngster coming with his newspapers, he's one of my best eel customers. Whenever a gentleman gives him a penny and takes no change, he comes here for a halfpenny-worth of eels. "Spoon 'em up big, guvnor". Fish on Fridays goes down with the Irish and on Saturday nights we often get a better class of customers . . . Although I say it, no finer fish can be got, not at Greenwich or anywhere else.'
    J. Thomson and Adolphe Smith, Street Life in London, 1876.

Other London specialities are jellied eels, which are eels cooked in stock which jells when cold; and hot eels served in a parsley broth with mashed potato. Several of these stalls and shops are now to be found in Islington, Bermondsey and parts of the East End. Eel-Pie Island in the Thames at Richmond was famous for a pie made with eel, parsley, sherry, shallots, butter and lemon all topped with puff pastry.

OYSTER CREAMS
The days have long past since Sam Weller in the *Pickwick Papers* was able to say: 'It's a wery remarkable circumstance, sir, that poverty and oysters always seem to go together.'

2 dozen oysters, either fresh or canned	4 tablespoons cream
3 separated eggs	1 cup fresh white breadcrumbs
a pinch of mace, salt and cayenne	

Chop up the oysters finely, reserving any liquor, then separate the eggs, beat the yolks, and mix with the oysters, breadcrumbs, cream and oyster juice. Add the seasonings and mix well. Whip up the egg-whites until stiff, then add to the mixture. Butter a 3-pint (2-l.) mould, or 6 individual ones, and put the mixture in, up to about two-thirds full. Stand in a *bain-marie* or pan of hot water and bake for 35 minutes if in one large dish, or 15 minutes if individual. Serve at once; or they can be served cold and masked with aspic jelly, poured on when the creams are cold.   Serves 6.
    This cream can also be made with mussels, cockles, or clams: or 2 cups (454 gr.) chopped prawns, lobster or crawfish.

Oyster, eel, whelk and mussel stall, possibly Drury Lane, or Whitechapel, c. 1876; photographer, J. Thomson.

STEAK AND KIDNEY PUDDING

Many of the famous London Clubs developed from the coffee houses (see pages 78, 93). It is possible that the coffee house in the photograph is the one mentioned by Dickens in A Tale of Two Cities, *but that may have been the still existing Cheshire Cheese, Wine Office Court, Fleet Street, a favourite meeting place for Dr Samuel Johnson. The Cheshire Cheese is still famous for its steak and kidney pudding which ranged from 50 to 80 lb. in weight, and took from 16 to 20 hours to boil : 'entombed there-in, beef-steaks, kidneys, oysters, larks, mushrooms and wondrous spices and gravies, the secret of which is only known to the compounder.' Other places in London which serve excellent steak and kidney puddings are Simpson's-in-the-Strand ; The Old Dr Butler's Head, Masons Avenue EC2, and Rule's Restaurant, Maiden Lane, WC2, whose chef, André Chion, kindly gave me the following recipe.*

As oysters have gone up in price since Dr Johnson used to feed his cat, Hodge, on them at 2d. a day, I have omitted them from this recipe, but more opulent readers can include a dozen. Where game is plentiful this recipe is excellent for hare, venison or elderly game birds used with a little beefsteak.

3 lb. (1·361 kg.) stewing steak, either rib, chuck or shin
1 lb. (454 gr.) ox kidney
1 small finely chopped or grated onion
½ lb. (227 gr.) chopped button mushrooms (optional)
1 tablespoon Worcestershire sauce
2 teaspoons chopped parsley
2 tablespoons flour
1 pint (2 cups) (0·57 l.) water or stock
salt and pepper

FOR THE CRUST
1 lb. (4 cups) (454 gr.) flour
2 oz. (1 cup) (57 gr.) fresh breadcrumbs
½ lb. (2 cups) (227 gr.) grated suet
½ pint (1 cup) (0·285 l.) water (approx.)
pinch of salt

First lightly grease a 4-pint (2·28-l.) pudding basin, then make the crust by mixing together the suet, flour, breadcrumbs and salt and stirring in the water until you have a smooth pliable dough. Turn out on to a floured board and line the basin with the dough (¼-in. thick), reserving enough for the top.

Remove any fat, bone or gristle from the meat and kidney and cut into 1-inch cubes, and roll the meat in the seasoned flour until it is coated. Peel the mushrooms and put all ingredients, layered, into the basin, adding the water last, and season well. Do not let the water come above half an inch from the top. Damp the edges, roll out the remaining crust and cover, pressing down the edges. Cover with greaseproof paper, then lay a large cloth over the top, tie with string and knot the four ends over the top. Steam over boiling water for 4-5 hours; longer cooking will only improve it. Remove paper and cloth before serving, and serve with a jug of boiling water, so that when the first slice is cut some water can be added before it is served. The gravy is so rich and luscious that quite a lot of water needs to be added.

Serves 6-8.

Groom's Coffee House, Fleet Street, 1899.

HITEBAIT, SOUCHET

Since medieval times it has been a summer custom to go by water to Greenwich, and a river boat still plies in the summer from Westminster Bridge and Charing Cross Pier, but alas the Souchet and the freshly caught whitebait dinners are a thing of the past, although frozen whitebait are available. Old Greenwich Fair in the Park was the scene of every variety of entertainment. 'The Fair began directly you landed from the ship "Torbay Tavern" up to the Park gates, and the road was bordered on either side with stalls, games, and handwaggons containing goods or refreshments of every description . . .'
G. Culver Budd,

Easter and Whitsun Fairs in and about old Greenwich, *1910.*

'Then won't I have a precious lark
Down One Tree Hill in Greenwich Park.'
Cruickshank, Comic Almanack.

'Gladstone at Greenwich
Ate his whitebait gaily,
Then ordered tea and shrimps,
And sent for Disraeli.
Benjamin Disraeli sent back word to say:
"I'm wanted in the City,
It's Lord Mayor's Day".'

WHITEBAIT are the small fry of the herring although sometimes small sprats are used as well. They used to be found in large quantities in the Thames and huge shoals were caught at Greenwich and Blackwall during July and August. Until 1895 Ministers of the Crown had a whitebait dinner provided by the Trafalgar Tavern in Greenwich (Lord Nelson's body was brought to Greenwich to lie in state), and the Opposition were provided with the same at the Old Ship Tavern.

At least $\frac{1}{2}$ lb. (227 gr.) whitebait should be allowed per person. Keep the whitebait in a cold place before using, then wash and dry them very thoroughly. Have enough seasoned flour in a large plastic bag, then shake a handful at a time in the flour. Do this just before frying, for they become soggy if left. Heat up oil in a deep-fryer until a faint blue haze comes from it, then fry a handful of whitebait at a time in a frying basket for 2 to 3 minutes. When ready, drain on paper or a rack and keep in a warm place until all are done, then put all the whitebait together into the frying basket for 1-2 minutes until crisp. Serve at once with salt, brown bread and butter and wedges of lemon. Iced champagne or punch was drunk with them. When served with cayenne pepper liberally sprinkled over them they are called Devilled Whitebait.

While waiting for the whitebait to be cooked, at Greenwich a fish soup called Souchet or Souchy (from the Flemish *Waterzootje*) was served. Souchet is a clear fish soup flavoured with parsley, peppercorns, a little onion and slices of lemon, and served with hot brown toast.

Swigg's Hotel for whitebait dinners, King William Walk, Greenwich, 1885.

ROAST BEEF WITH YORKSHIRE PUDDING

In the eighteenth century, London was the envy of many people in Paris for its superb taverns and chop houses where foods such as oysters, turtle soup, toasted cheese and vast chops and steaks could be got, all at reasonable prices. The London Tavern at which John Farley (author of The London Art of Cookery, *1783) was chief cook went on for a full hundred years. The first public restaurant in Paris was opened in 1782 and was called 'La Grande Taverne de Londres' after the London Tavern. Rule's Restaurant in Maiden Lane (still going strong) was opened in 1798 by Thomas Rule and his three sons, mainly as an oyster house: 'And the three young Rules rush wildly about; With dozens of oysters and pewters of stout.' Simpson's-in-the-Strand was opened in 1828 as a 'home of chess', later known as the 'Grand Cigar Divan'; smokers and chess players sat on divans or sofas to play. In 1848 John Simpson joined as a caterer and the building was rebuilt and opened as in the photograph. Mr Simpson introduced the excellently cooked meals and the idea of wheeling the hot joints on trolleys to the diner. Ever since, this has been a well-known feature of Simpson's. Other famous dishes there, are steak and kidney pudding (page 45), roast mutton (page 59) and Syrup Roly-Poly (page 25). 'At a Coffee House you may dine for 2/6d, and there is also a Cigar Divan in the Strand . . . where you may lounge in the evening and have admirable coffee, a cigar and newspaper to read in a splendid well warmed room for 1/–.*

William Hone, Table Book, *1831*

'Oh, the roast beef of England,
And, old England's roast beef.'
Henry Fielding, *The Grub Street Opera.*

5-6 lb. (2·270-2·720 kg.) sirloin beef
black pepper, rosemary, if liked

YORKSHIRE PUDDING, recipe kindly given by Mr R. Smythe of Simpson's-in-the-Strand.

2 eggs
4 oz. (1 cup) (114 gr.) flour
½ pint (1 cup) (0·285 l.) milk

1 teaspoon olive oil
salt and pepper

Make the batter for the Yorkshire pudding when you first put in the meat and let it stand to get the air into it.

Put the beef into a roasting pan with a sprig of rosemary and black pepper, and put into a hot oven (400°F.) without any fat, for ½ hour, then reduce the heat to 350°F. and roast for 20 minutes to the pound, plus 10 minutes over, for underdone beef and 25 minutes to the pound, plus 10 minutes, for well-done. Baste about 3 times, with the pan juices.

TO MAKE THE PUDDING

First separate the yolks from whites of the eggs and well beat the yolks. Add the flour gradually to the yolks, then thin it down with the oil and milk, and add the salt. Beat well until like thick cream. Leave to stand until the meat is about ½ hour from being cooked. Then stir in the stiffly beaten whites and mix well. Have ready a pan with about 1 inch of piping hot beef dripping in it, and pour in the batter. It should sizzle up when it goes in. Put the meat on a lower shelf and the pudding on the top one. Cook for about ½ hour, until it is golden brown and well-risen. Serve the pudding at once with the meat and with horseradish sauce. Enough for 6-8.

POTTED SHRIMPS

Pleasure gardens developed from a mixture of the tea gardens and the concert rooms of the eighteenth century, the most famous being the Vauxhall Gardens which continued well into the nineteenth century. Two other famous 'Gardens' overlapped the Vauxhall by many years, namely the Cremorne Gardens in Chelsea (the centre of which is now marked by the four chimneys of the Chelsea Power Station) and the Surrey Gardens in Southwark, both of which went on until the 1870s. They were not just gardens, for the Surrey also had a zoo and a concert hall, called the Surrey Music Hall. Spectacular acts were performed: in the 1840s General Tom Thumb appeared in the Surrey Gardens, also Blackmore the wire-walker, and the Heptaplaspcoptron, a wondrous device with an arrangement of objects which were reflected seven times. These gardens were frequented by all classes: Horace Walpole in his letters writes, 'Here [at Vauxhall] we picked up Lord Granby, arrived very drunk from Jenny's Whim' (a garden near Ebury Bridge). They were originally built to be used at night and lost a lot of their glamour by daytime opening. Dickens, writing in Sketches by Boz, 1837, *found the gardens to be 'Nothing but a combination of roughly painted boards.'*

'That, the Moorish Tower,' he cries, 'that wooden shed with a door in the centre, and daubs of crimson and yellow all round, like a gigantic watch-case! That, the place where night after night we had beheld the undaunted Mr Blackmore make his terrific ascent, surrounded by flames of fire and peals of artillery . . .'

Other amusements were 'Hollands, punch, claret drawn from the wood at 3/6d. a quart. Skittles and quoits, accompanied of course, with pipes and tobacco, offered their fascination to the male customers; while the ladies and juveniles were beguiled with cakes and ale, tea and shrimps, strawberries and cream, fruit pies, syllabubs, swings and mazes, admiring the flowers . . . the currants and gooseberries that spread their alluring charms in every path.' It was also a favourite rendezvous for lovers, a day's pleasure being considered the most enticing enjoyment that could be offered. ' . . . the hungry perspiring pleasure-seeker would indulge in a "shilling ordinary", to which, by the way, a known good appetite would not be admitted under eighteenpence!'

POTTED SHRIMPS (served with hot, dry toast)

This recipe is made with the very small shrimps *(Crangon vulgaris)*, but larger shrimps or prawns can be used if chopped. Lobster, crawfish or crab can also be used to advantage.

1 lb. (2 cups) (454 gr.) picked boiled shrimps	6 oz. (¾ cup) (170 gr.) butter
1 teaspoon ground mace	a pinch grated nutmeg
a good pinch cayenne pepper	freshly ground pepper

Heat two-thirds of the butter in a saucepan with the seasonings and when hot add the shrimps, stirring well. Heat and stir them so that the shrimps get impregnated with the spicy butter, but do not let them boil. Put into small pots, then heat the remaining butter and when it stops foaming but is not brown, pour over the top of the pots and leave until set.

A Moorish Pavilion at Surrey Gardens, Southwark, c. 1871.

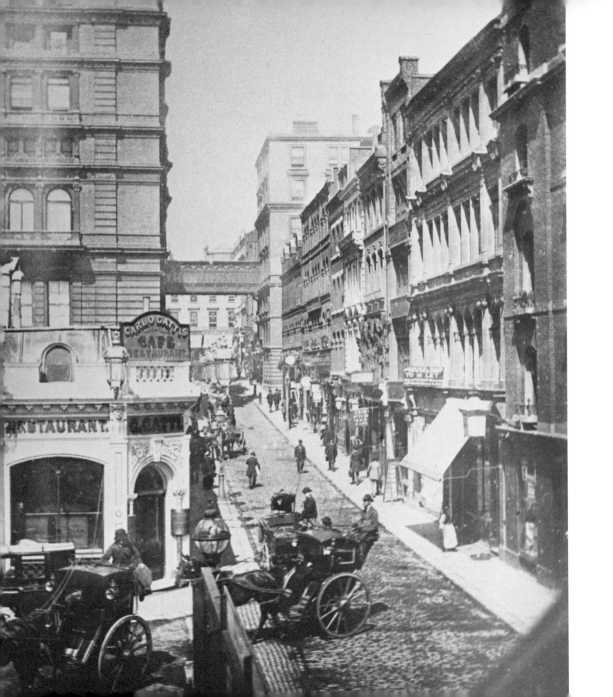

BRAISED DUCK

The Gatti brothers, as well as owning a popular restaurant, also owned or managed several music-halls, the Alhambra being one of them. The restaurant therefore became a well known rendezvous for theatre-goers. The first music-hall founded by Carlo Gatti in 1865 was in Westminster Bridge Road, and known as Gatti's 'in the Road'. However, when Charing Cross Station was built in 1863, a pub was built in one of the arches underneath and called 'The Arches'. This was taken over by Gatti and turned into a music-hall called 'Gatti's in the Arches', later to be the famous Hungerford music-hall. This survived until 1910 when it became a cinema, but in 1937 the actor Harold Scott presented a Victorian style cabaret in the same premises, called 'Ridgeway's, Late Joys'. In 1946 it became the home of the Players' Theatre.

BRAISED DUCK WITH PEAS

A dish remembered with pleasure by the oldest living member of my family at Gatti's. It combines both English and Italian cooking in a most successful way.

1 duck about 4-5 lb. (2 kg.)
4 oz. (½ cup) (114 gr.) butter or oil
1 tablespoon flour, seasoned with salt and pepper
1 pint (2 cups) (0·57 l.) stock, preferably made from the giblets
2 tablespoons Marsala or sweet Vermouth

1 lb. (4 cups) (454 gr.) shelled fresh green peas
2 small chopped lettuce
1 tablespoon of mixed chopped mint and marjoram
a pinch of grated nutmeg
1 egg-yolk beaten with 2 tablespoons cream

Heat up the oil or butter in a metal casserole and rub the duck all over with the seasoned flour, then brown it on all sides in the hot fat over a low flame letting it sauté gently with the lid on. Then pour off any surplus fat and add the Marsala or Vermouth, letting it burn out before adding the stock and the mixed herbs. Season to taste and simmer very gently for about 20 minutes. Then add the peas and lettuce and again cover and simmer very slowly until the peas and duck are both cooked and tender. This should be about 1 hour. Shake the pan from time to time so that it does not stick, but avoid taking off the lid too much. Add the nutmeg and adjust seasoning. Beat up the egg-yolk and cream and with the duck off the heat stir this in, mixing very well all the time. Let it heat up, but do not let it boil. Serve with the duck in the middle of a warmed dish and the vegetables and sauce around the outside. For easy serving the duck can be disjointed when removed from the sauce and heated gently in a low oven before adding to the peas and sauce.

Serves 4.

Gatti's Restaurant, Villiers Street entrance, Charing Cross, c. 1890.

CHRISTMAS PUDDING AND BRANDY BUTTER

The pudding now known as Christmas Pudding did not appear in its present form until about 1675 (the Puritans had condemned it as a 'wicked luxury'). Before that date it was more of a porridge with suet, dried fruits and spices added; in fact another way of using the dried fruits and spices which had been stored against the long winter.

Christmas puddings should be made about the beginning of November, but not later than three weeks before Christmas. They will last a full year and be only the better for it. See also Mincepies, page 3. The Hyde Park Hotel has been noted for its Christmas puddings for over forty years.

These amounts make two puddings to fill two 2-pint (approx. 1¼-l.) basins.

4 oz. (1 cup) (114 gr.) flour
½ teaspoon salt
2 teaspoons each: mixed spice, cinnamon and nutmeg
2 oz. (½ cup) (57 gr.) ground almonds
8 oz. (1 cup) (227 gr. brown sugar
8 oz. (2 cups) (227 gr.) grated suet
14 oz. (8 cups) (397 gr.) fresh breadcrumbs

6 eggs
½ lb. (227 gr.) each of: seedless raisins, sultanas, currants, glacé cherries
½ lb. (227 gr.) chopped mixed candied peel
¼ pint (½ cup) (0·142 l.) brandy or rum
½ pint stout or Guinness (0·285 l.)
4 oz. (1 cup) (114 gr.) mixed walnuts and almonds

1 orange, rind and juice
1 grated apple
1 grated carrot

Sort out the dried fruit, and pick it over, then grate the apple, carrot, and the orange peel. Mix all together with the dry ingredients, beat the eggs well, and add with the other liquids Stir well (it is considered lucky to stir the pudding and wish at the same time) and add a lucky charm or a small silver piece to the mixture. (It can at this stage be left overnight without coming to any harm.) Grease the 2 deep pudding bowls and divide the mixture between them. Cover with greased grease-proof paper and then with foil and tie down securely. The old method of using a large napkin and tying that down, is better, for the loops knotted over the top give one a handle to lift the pudding up with. Either steam, or put into boiling water up to the rim, and cook for 6 hours. Resteam or reboil for a further 2 hours on Christmas Day.   1 pudding serves about 8.

BRANDY BUTTER

Cream 8 oz. (1 cup) (227 gr.) butter with half the quantity of sugar. When thoroughly mixed add 4 tablespoons of brandy gradually, beating after each addition until it is white and foamy. Pile up in a dish and chill to harden. Rum butter is made the same way, except that brown soft sugar is used, and it is finished with a squeeze of lemon juice.   Serves 8.

In the new ballroom of the Hyde Park Hotel, c. 1912; photographer, H. Walter Barnett.

BRAISED STEAK, DEVILLED KIDNEYS

'Vernon, the butcher Cumberland,
Wolfe, Hawke,
Prince Ferdinand, Granby, Burgoyne,
Keppell, Howe,
Evil and good have had their tithe,
And fill'd the signposts then, as
Wellesley now.'

(Wellesley is the family name of the Duke of Wellington)

BRAISED STEAK

3 lb. (1·362 kg.) stewing steak, about 1 inch thick and free from fat, bone and gristle	4 medium onions, sliced
2 tablespoons dripping or oil	1 lb. (454 gr.) peeled tomatoes or equivalent can
1 tablespoon Worcestershire sauce	1 teaspoon sugar
6 pickled walnuts or gherkins	a pinch of mace, salt and pepper
	4 tablespoons water

Heat the dripping or oil and fry the steak, cut into large serving pieces, quickly on both sides, then put into a casserole. Then fry the onions in the same fat until they are golden brown, and put them on top of the steak. Season with the salt, pepper, sugar and mace, and mix the Worcestershire sauce with the water and pour over. Then add the peeled tomatoes, roughly chopped, and season again. If using canned tomatoes the juice can be added, but halve the amount of water. Cover, and cook in a slow oven (250°F.) for about 2 hours. Five minutes before serving add the sliced pickled walnuts or gherkins. Serves 4-6.

The Wellington Arms, Shepherd's Bush Green, c. 1888.

DEVILLED KIDNEYS

12 lambs' kidneys
2 tablespoons oil or dripping

FOR THE DEVIL

1 tablespoon dry mustard powder	2 teaspoons mushroom or tomato ketchup
1 tablespoon flour	2 tablespoons chutney
2 teaspoons Worcestershire sauce	4 oz. ($\frac{1}{2}$ cup) (114 gr.) butter

First heat the oil or dripping, and fry the skinned, defatted and halved kidneys on both sides for about 5 minutes, then keep them warm but do not let them overcook. To make the devil, mash the butter on a plate and work the flour into it, then add all the other ingredients and mix well. Light the grill and transfer the kidneys to the dish they will be served from, cover with the devil sauce and grill until it is melted. Cutlets, steaks, cold joints of cooked chicken, or meat can also be done this way.

Serves 4.

'Every man must have experienced that, when he has got deep into his third bottle, his palate acquires a degree of torpidity and his stomach is seized with a certain craving, which seems to demand a stimulant to the powers of both. The provocatives used on such an occasion, an ungrateful world has combined to term devils.'

Dr William Kitchiner, *The Cook's Oracle,* 1817.

STUFFED SHOULDER OF LAMB

Almost all pubs sold hot meals at this time, the most popular dishes being chops, steaks, or a 'cut off the joint with two veg'. Including soup and a pudding, a shilling would have been the usual price. Snacks such as pickled onions and cheese were often put on the bar counter, and provided free, for the customers.

STUFFED SHOULDER OF LAMB WITH ONION SAUCE

1 boned shoulder lamb or mutton about 4-5 lb. (approx. 2 kg.)
stock or red wine

2 tablespoons mutton dripping
black pepper
a shake of seasoned flour

FOR THE STUFFING
2 rashers chopped bacon
2 finely chopped shallots or onions
1 teaspoon chopped parsley
½ teaspoon chopped rosemary or thyme
rind and juice of ½ lemon
4 tablespoons breadcrumbs soaked in 2 tablespoons milk
salt and pepper

FOR THE SAUCE*
3 large sliced onions
2 tablespoons butter
1 heaped tablespoon flour
½ pint (1 cup) (0·285 l.) milk
a pinch of nutmeg
¼ pint (½ cup) (0·142 l.) cream

*Redcurrant jelly or mint sauce may be served instead: and when the meat is cold Cumberland Sauce, page 84, is excellent.

Mix all the stuffing ingredients together and put into the cavity left by the bone, then either sew up or secure with small skewers. If any stuffing is left over then make into small balls, and roast for the last ½ hour around the joint. Put the meat into a roasting tin, dust with pepper and add the dripping. Bake in a moderate oven (350°F.) for 20 minutes to the pound, basting from time to time. 15 minutes before it is ready, shake over the seasoned flour and sprinkle the top with a dash of cold water. This 'froths' the skin and makes it crisp. Pour off any excess fat and add a cup of either stock or red wine to the pan juices. Put the joint on a warm dish and keep warm, then boil up the gravy until it is reduced by half on top of the stove.

TO MAKE THE SAUCE
Start when the joint is about half cooked. Slice the onions very thinly, then melt the butter in a saucepan and slowly fry them in it until they are soft but in no way brown. Sprinkle the flour over, then add the milk, stirring so that there are no lumps. Add the nutmeg and season to taste. When the sauce is ready to serve stir in the cream, but do not boil it. Serve hot, separately, with the meat.

Serves about 10.

Before opening time in the saloon bar of the White Horse, Shepherd's Bush, c. 1910.

59

CARPET-BAG STEAKS

Many London Clubs became famous for their food, such as the Sublime Society of Beefsteaks (The Beefsteak Club) of which Rule 4 was: 'That beefsteaks shall be the only meat for dinner and the broiling begin at two of the clock on each day of meeting, and the table cloth be removed at half an hour after three.' Their motto is: 'When 'tis done, 'twere well it were done quickly.' The Reform Club, founded in 1832, was fortunate to acquire the services of the famous chef Alexis Soyer in 1837. He was not only a master chef, but a writer of many books, an inventor and a humanitarian noted for his work during the famine in Ireland and in the Crimea. He died in 1858 at the age of 49. Florence Nightingale wrote 'Soyer's death is a great disaster', but he never received any public recognition for his work. See also pages 15 and 93.

> *'The dear old street of clubs and cribs,*
> *As north and south it stretches,*
> *Still seems to smack of Rolliad squibs,*
> *And Gilray's fiercer sketches.'*
> *Anon.*

CARPET-BAG STEAKS

Soyer liked his steaks to be at least 1 inch thick, and preferred rump to fillet. He cooked them over charcoal, allowing 10 minutes altogether for cooking time over a very hot fire. This would be very rare steak.

2 lb. (1 kg. approx.) rump or fillet steak in one piece
½ lb. (227 gr.) pâté de foie gras *or* 12 oysters
4 oz. (½ cup) (114 gr.) butter
freshly ground black pepper
a bunch of watercress
1 tablespoon chopped parsley
2 tablespoons olive oil
1 lb. (454 gr.) mushrooms

Slit the steak along the middle, but do not cut it right through, so as to make a 'pocket'. Sprinkle the inside of the pocket with black pepper and stuff with either the pâté or the oysters, then either tie up or secure well with small skewers. Rub with half the butter and sprinkle again with pepper over the top. Preheat the oven to 425°F. and meanwhile put the cleaned mushrooms into a casserole with the olive oil and parsley, seasoning to taste. Cover and put into the hot oven on the upper shelf. After ½ hour cooking put them down to the bottom shelf. While they are cooking heat the rest of the butter in a thick pan and quickly sear the steak on both sides, then put it (with the butter) into a roasting tin on the top shelf of the oven, for about 15-20 minutes if liked rare, or about 30 minutes for a well-done steak. Remove the string or skewers before serving, put on to a warmed serving dish with its juices, and garnish with watercress. Serve the mushrooms in their juice as a side dish.

An excellent amount for 2.

TOMATO SAUCE, MUSHROOM KETCHUP

Since the early 1840s the coffee stall has been a feature of London night life. Henry Mayhew writes in 1851: 'The best "pitch" in London is supposed to be at the corner of Duke Street, Oxford Street. The proprietor of that stall is said to take a full 30/- of a morning, in halfpence. Those that come out at midnight are for the convenience of the "night-walkers"—"fast gentlemen" and loose girls; and those that come out in the morning are for the accommodation of the working men.' Nowadays coffee stalls are mainly used by taxi drivers, parties returning from late dances, and night-shift workers. Tea, coffee or hot Bovril can be bought; pies, sandwiches, biscuits, and in some places, chipped potatoes and hot baked beans are sold, and can be liberally covered with a bottled sauce or ketchup to taste.

TOMATO SAUCE

8 lb. (3·630 kg.) tomatoes, peeled

1 lb. (454 g.) peeled and chopped onions

6 medium cloves garlic

½ pint (1 cup) (0·285 l.) white vinegar

1 tablespoon dry mustard powder

1½ lb. (3 cups) (681 gr.) sugar

1 teaspoon each: mixed spice, paprika, ginger

½ teaspoon cayenne pepper

1½ tablespoons salt

Skin the tomatoes by immersing them in boiling water, then chop coarsely. Peel and chop the onions finely and crush the garlic, then combine both vegetables in a large saucepan and simmer for about 20 minutes. Add the vinegar, mustard, salt and spices, mix well and simmer again for a further hour. Remove from the heat, add the sugar, then heat gently until the sugar is dissolved and boil gently for about 15–20 minutes. Pour into hot, sterilized jars and seal at once.

Makes about 7 lb. (3 kg.).

MUSHROOM KETCHUP

6 lb. (2·720 kg.) mushrooms

6 oz. (⅔ cup) (170 gr.) salt

1 tablespoon chopped onion, *or* 3 crushed garlic cloves

2 tablespoons soy sauce

1 pint (2 cups) (0·57 l.) vinegar which has been boiled with a teaspoon each of whole cloves, cinnamon, all-spice and ginger, then strained

First boil up the vinegar, leave to get cold with the whole spices, then strain it and reserve the liquid. Chop the mushrooms, sprinkle with salt and leave for 24-36 hours. Add the vinegar and the onion to the mushrooms with their liquor and simmer gently for about 3 hours. Strain through muslin, add the soy sauce and bottle in hot, sterilized bottles, with screwcaps if possible. Makes about 3 pints (approx. 1¾ l.).

FILLETS OF BEEF

The name Kensington comes from 'Chenesitun' which indicates a connection with Chenesi, a personal name in Saxon times. This name was also spelt Cynesige, and the English Place Names Society gives the derivation as 'Cynesige's farm', although other sources give it as 'sons of Cynesige'. Kensington is now famous for the many museums it houses, and also as a shopping centre.

FILLETS OF BEEF WITH MADEIRA SAUCE

Sirloin, rump, T-bone or Porterhouse steak can also be used.

4 thick steaks
2 tablespoons butter or olive oil
black pepper

FOR THE SAUCE
2 tablespoons butter
2 medium chopped onions
2 tablespoons flour
salt and pepper

½ pint (1 cup) (0·285 l.) stock or white wine
12 sliced button mushrooms
6 tablespoons Madeira

First make the sauce by melting the butter in a thick saucepan until it is very hot, then put in the sliced onions and cook them until they are an even pale gold colour. Then add the flour, stirring until the mixture is an even brown. Add the stock or wine gradually, stirring each time, until it is all used up and the mixture like a thick white sauce. Season to taste, then either strain it or purée in a blender. Leave to one side to keep warm. Trim the steaks and brush over with butter or oil and sprinkle with black pepper. Either cook under a hot grill or fry in the butter or oil in a thick pan. Cook according to taste, and when ready transfer to a warmed dish and keep warm. Fry the button mushrooms in the pan juices and when just soft but in no way brown, add the sauce, stir well, and when well mixed add the Madeira, stirring between each spoonful. Simmer for a few minutes, then serve over or around the steaks.

Serves 4.

Kensington High Street decorated for Queen Victoria's Golden Jubilee, 1887.

BOILED CHICKEN AND CUCUMBER SAUCE

1 boiling chicken about $4\frac{1}{2}$ lb. (2 kg.)
1 tablespoon each, coarsely chopped tarragon and parsley
salt and pepper

FOR THE SAUCE
1 cucumber about 8 inches long, peeled and chopped into
  1-inch pieces
1 large lettuce heart
1 small sliced onion
1 tablespoon flour
1 tablespoon chopped tarragon (or parsley if tarragon is
  not available)
2 oz. ($\frac{1}{4}$ cup) (57 gr.) butter
juice of 1 lemon or 2 tablespoons sherry
2 tablespoons cream
a few sprigs of watercress
approx. 1 pint (2 cups) (0·57 l.) chicken stock

Stuff the tarragon and parsley into the body of the bird and put it into a saucepan with water to $\frac{2}{3}$ up, add salt and pepper, cover, bring to the boil and let it simmer slowly for 2 to 3 hours, depending on when it becomes tender. In a separate saucepan melt half the butter and very lightly fry the chopped peeled cucumber, sliced onion and the lettuce heart, which has been roughly pulled to pieces. Do not let them brown at all, but when they are all soft stir in the flour, and let it cook for 1 minute. Add the stock from the chicken, gradually, stirring well to avoid lumps, then add the chopped tarragon, and let it simmer until the vegetables are tender, which should be about 20 minutes. Then add the lemon juice or sherry. About 5 minutes before serving the chicken add the rest of the butter in small pieces, the chopped watercress and the cream. Stir well, keep it hot, but do not reboil once the cream is in for fear of curdling. Skin the chicken before sending to table and pour the sauce over the top. Garnish with more watercress and wedges of lemon.

Croquet at Rivercourt (now 36 Upper Mall), Chiswick, 1869. The ruins of Catherine of Braganza's (Queen to Charles II) Banqueting House is in the grounds of this fine old house.

LAMB CHOPS

'Come, Come, Come and make eyes at me,
  Down at the Old Bull and Bush'.
            Harry Tilzer, music hall song
              sung by Miss Florrie Forde

Hampstead has been famous for its taverns since the seventeenth century: the Upper Flask Tavern (now a private house), at the corner of East Heath Road and East Mount, was the meeting place of the well-known Kit-Kat Club, which included among its members such wits as Sir Richard Steele, Addison, Congreve, Pope, Vanbrugh and Sir Richard Blackmore. 'The Spaniards' is reputed to have been a haunt of the highwayman Dick Turpin, and was also the scene of Mrs Bardell's tea party in The Pickwick Papers. *Jack Straw's Castle is said to be the place where Jack Straw, second in command to Wat Tyler, encamped with his tattered followers, when they advanced on London in 1381, although it was then only a hovel. The 'Bull and Bush' was also visited by Addison and Steele, and in the popular tea-gardens Hogarth planted a mulberry tree, which is huge now: it has often been a haunt of painters, for Morland and Constable (who lived in Well Walk) found it an agreeable meeting place. 'When shall we see you at sweet Hampstead again?' wrote Constable to a friend. Charles Dickens was a frequent visitor to Hampstead and wrote of Jack Straw's Castle in a letter to John Forster: 'You don't feel disposed, do you, to muffle yourself up, and start off for a good brisk walk over Hampstead Heath? I know a good house where we can have a red-hot chop for dinner, and a glass of good wine.'*

'Down at the Old Bull and Bush', Bank Holiday, c. 1902

LAMB CHOPS AND TOMATO SAUCE
(see also page 63)

'Chops and Tomata sauce, Yours, Pickwick'.
                    The Pickwick Papers.

4 thick loin chops   black pepper

FOR THE SAUCE

1 lb. (454 gr.) peeled tomatoes or equivalent canned   2 shallots or small onions

3 slices chopped ham   1 clove garlic

a good pinch cayenne pepper   3 tablespoons vinegar

salt and pepper   1 bay leaf

Peel and chop the tomatoes and the shallots then add them to the diced ham, garlic and bay leaf. Cook very slowly for about 1½ hours until they become a purée. Remove the bay leaf, then put through a sieve or liquidize, and add the cayenne, vinegar and seasonings. Dust the chops with black pepper and grill to your taste under a hot grill. Serve the sauce hot.

Cutlets or Chops are also excellent served with Onion sauce (page 59) or Madeira sauce (page 64).

Pies

'The itinerant trade in pies is one of the most ancient of the street callings of London. The meat pies are made of beef or mutton; the fish pies of eels; the fruit of apples, currants, gooseberries, plums, damsons, cherries, raspberries or rhubarb, according to the season—and occasionally of mincemeat. Summer fairs and races are the best places for pie-men . . . the pieman makes a practise of "looking in" at all the taverns on his way. "Here's all 'ot" . . . "toss or buy! up and win'em!" "If it wasn't for tossing we shouldn't sell one." To toss the pieman is a favourite pastime with costermongers' boys and all that class; if the pieman wins the toss, he receives a penny without giving the pie: if he lose he hands it over for nothing. Gentlemen "out on the spree" . . . will frequently toss when they don't want the pies, and when they win they will amuse themselves by throwing the pies at one another, or at me.' Henry Mayhew, *London Labour and the London Poor*, 1851.

HOT-WATER CRUST FOR RAISED PIES
Hot-water crust is not difficult to make but it must be done quickly before the lard 'sets'. It is possible to buy modern versions of the old metal hinged moulds, which are removed for the last few minutes of baking to brown the sides. To make a pie large enough for 4-5 people, about 6 inches across and 6 inches high:

12 oz. (3 cups) (340 gr.) plain flour	¼ pint (½ cup) (0·142 l.) warm water
½ teaspoon salt	egg for glazing
4 oz. (½ cup) (114 gr.) slightly warm lard	

Sieve the flour with the salt and rub in a quarter of the lard. Melt the remaining lard in the hot water, make a well in the flour and pour in the hot liquid. Mix with a knife blade until it forms lumps, then knead quickly with the hands. It must be done quickly as the dough must be warm when moulded. Set aside one third for the lid (covered with a warm cloth). Roll out the remaining pastry, put a 2-lb. (1-kg.) warmed jam jar in the middle and mould the pastry up around this to about 6 inches deep. Turn on its side and roll to and fro to smooth the sides. Lift out the jar, and fill with whatever meat, fish, etc. you are using. It must be well-chopped, either raw or partly cooked, a few chopped herbs and seasoning. In the case of veal and ham pies a sliced hard-boiled egg is added. Fill to about ½ inch of the top, turn the edge over slightly, then roll out the lid, damp the edges and press on securely, pinching or cutting the edges. Cut a neat hole in the lid, and make a small leaf or rosette from the pastry to cover it, but do not press it on. Brush with beaten egg all over, then bake in the middle of a moderate oven (350°F.), reducing the heat after the first 1 hour to 275°F. If using meat or fish, have ready about ½ cup of aspic which will jelly when cold. Pour this in through the cut in the top, when cooked, replace the rosette and leave until completely cold and set. The same fillings can be put into shortcrust pastry (page 109) either using a deep pie dish or making into pasties.

CELERY

Celery is a favourite English vegetable and is used frequently in many ways. A good Stilton or Cheddar cheese is not complete without the curled celery standing in a glass of cold water on the table. To curl celery, chop off the top leaves at an angle with a sharp knife, then pull the strings which lurk in between the ridges down the stalk sharply. This will result in the top curling over: it also means that the stringy part of the celery has been removed. The thick stalks should be cut into thin slices downwards, for convenient eating, and left to stand in ice-cold water for some hours before serving. Do not remove the hard root at the bottom, but trim and clean it: dipped into salt, which is put on the plate, it is the best part. Curls of celery about two inches long make an excellent garnish for a clear soup; they do not need cooking if they are thin enough and should be added just before serving.

CELERY SOUP

1 large trimmed head of celery
½ pint (1 cup) (0·285 l.) chicken stock
1 pint (2 cups) (0·57 l.) milk
½ pint (1 cup) (0·285 l.) cream
1 small sliced onion
1 tablespoon flour rubbed in 1 tablespoon butter
salt, pepper and a pinch nutmeg

Chop the celery into small pieces, then put it in a saucepan with the onion and the stock and simmer for ½ hour, then season to taste and add the milk. Let it come to the boil and simmer until it is tender, then either sieve or liquidize. Mix the butter and flour together, heat up the soup, and stir into the flour mixture, stirring until the soup has thickened. Finally stir in the cream, reheat, but do not reboil.

Serves 6.

CELERY SAUCE was popular with roast or boiled poultry and braised veal. It is made in the same way as the soup omitting the milk, but adding the cream as above.

Cold boiled celery makes a good salad with game or poultry when dressed with oil and vinegar; when hot it is excellent served with English Butter Sauce, page 75.

Taking the air in Kensington Gardens, c. 1895.

HADDOCK WITH ENGLISH BUTTER SAUCE

'Belin a King of the Britons, about 400 years before Christ's nativity builded this gate, and named it Belingsgate after his own calling.'

Geoffrey of Monmouth, c. 1140.

Billingsgate has been a fish market since 1699 and for many years the porters were known for their ribald and coarse speech.

HADDOCK WITH ENGLISH BUTTER SAUCE (also for hake, turbot, brill, cod, etc.)

English butter sauce is now almost forgotten, but when well-made can hold its own with a Hollandaise. Once made, it can be flavoured in many ways: chopped hard-boiled eggs with anchovy essence; chopped fennel or other herbs; lemon juice or sherry, also crab or finely chopped prawns or lobster. It can also be used for sweet puddings when sugar, nutmeg and a little wine are added as flavouring. In the nineteenth century it was served with meats and poultry as well as with many kinds of fish, such as salmon, trout or the rare char and shad.

4 thick fish steaks or fillets	1 pint (2 cups) (0·57 l.)
salt	water or preferably fish
a sprig of parsley or fennel	stock made from the
	trimmings or bones

Put the fish into the water or stock with salt to taste and the herbs. Cover the top with buttered paper, bring very gently to the boil and let it simmer slowly for about 20 minutes if the steaks are thick, or for only 10 minutes if using fillets. Lift the fish out, remove the skin, and keep warm in a low oven.

FOR THE SAUCE

6 oz. ($\frac{3}{4}$ cup) (170 gr.) butter	1 heaped tablespoon (28 gr.)
$\frac{1}{2}$ pint (1 cup) (0·285 l.) water	flour
a little ground nutmeg	salt and pepper

It is best to make the sauce in a double boiler as if it boils the butter is likely to oil. In the event of this happening add a teaspoon of cold water and beat well. Have the water in the bottom of the boiler hot, but not boiling, then in the top section mix the flour, pepper and nutmeg together with the water so that it is a smooth paste. When it is hot and just cooked, add the butter cut into small pieces and either stir well with a wooden spoon or beat with a wire whisk until all the butter is used up, the sauce creamy and slightly thickened. Add whatever flavouring you choose, and stir in salt to taste just before serving. Do not leave it to stand over boiling water or it will oil, but it will keep for about $\frac{1}{2}$ hour over hot water. Beat well before serving. Some recipes add a tablespoon of thick cream when the butter is used up, but this destroys the pure flavour. Serve the sauce over the fish and garnish with fresh parsley.

Serves 4.

Fish porters at Billingsgate Market, c. 1902; photographer, Paul Martin.

STUFFED ROAST VEAL WITH ANCHOVY SAUCE

Adapted from Cassell's *Dictionary of Cookery*, 1877.

Holborn Viaduct was one of the first 'flyovers' and was built between 1867 and when it was opened by Queen Victoria on 6th November 1869, the same day as the new Blackfriars Bridge. It is 1,400 feet long and 80 feet wide with bronze statues representing, on the south side, Commerce and Agriculture and, on the north side, Science and Fine Art. The bridge crosses the 'lost' River Fleet. Adjoining the viaduct was built a large ornate hotel, called the Holborn Viaduct Hotel, which was noted for its good food. It was from the nearby Holborn Station that the East End hop-pickers left for the hop fields of Kent.

> 'Old fish and young flesh wolde I have ful fain,
> Better is, quote he, a pyke than a pickerel
> And bet than old beef, is the tendre veal.'
>
> Geoffrey Chaucer, *c.* 1370

4¼ lb. (2 kg.) boned shoulder veal
4 tablespoons olive oil or butter
a sprig of rosemary
pepper

FOR THE STUFFING
1 cup fresh breadcrumbs or 4 large crustless slices
3 tablespoons milk
1 small chopped bacon rasher
salt and pepper
rind and juice of ½ lemon
1 tablespoon mixed chopped parsley and lemon thyme
a pinch of mace

FOR THE SAUCE
2 filleted canned anchovies
1 minced shallot or small onion
¼ pint (½ cup) (0·142 l.) stock
2 teaspoons lemon juice
4 tablespoons port
a nut of butter rolled with 2 teaspoons flour (*beurre manié*)

First make the stuffing by soaking the breadcrumbs or bread in the milk until it has been absorbed. Then mix with a fork, and break up if you have used the slices. Add the chopped herbs, lemon rind and juice, the chopped bacon rasher and seasonings and mix well. Put this into the cavity of the boned joint, then tie up securely. Put into a roasting tin with the olive oil or butter, chop the rosemary over the top and season with freshly ground pepper. Put into a preheated moderate oven (350° F.) and roast for 25 minutes to the pound, basting from time to time.

About ½ hour before the joint is ready, prepare the sauce. Chop the anchovies finely and put into a small saucepan with the shallot and the stock, then boil for about 15 minutes until the anchovy is dissolved. Strain it into another pan, then add the lemon juice, and port, bring to the boil and let it simmer for a few minutes. Well mix the butter into the flour and add this to the sauce, stirring well until it has thickened slightly. Remove the joint from the pan and put on to a warmed dish and keep warm. Pour off any excess fat then add the sauce to the pan juices, stir well, and boil up on top of the stove, mixing thoroughly. When it has reduced slightly, put into a warmed gravy boat, and serve separately with the joint.   Serves 8.

'Seeing the sights in London', Holborn Viaduct under construction, c. 1868.

BISHOP

The first coffee house was opened in London in 1652 in St Michael's Alley, Cornhill. The people who went to coffee houses formed themselves into coteries; Lloyd's of London grew out of a coffee house. Sir Richard Steele, writing about 1712 in The Tatler *said: 'I date all gallantry from White's; all poetry from Will's; all foreign and domestic news from St James's and all learned articles from the Grecian.' However, Swift said the worst conversation he ever heard in his life was at Will's Coffee House 'where the wits (as they were called)' used to assemble. Garraway's Coffee House was the first place in England to serve tea, in about 1660. Pepys records having drunk 'a cup of tea (a China drink) of which I had never drunk before', 25th September, 1660. Coffee houses also sold food and by the early nineteenth century were more or less frequented by people of quality.*

Now a private house, one of the earliest coffee houses in London, Don Saltero's was started by the Irish servant of Sir Hans Sloane (himself an Irishman) called James Salter in about 1717. Admiral Munden home from years of Spanish service dubbed him Don Saltero, a title he carried to his death. He was a placid, neat little man who had followed many trades until he found his vocation as a tavern keeper. Above the coffee house was a freak museum known as the 'Knackatory'. It was a great meeting place for many famous people such as Swift, Steele, Pennant, Smollett, Addison, and Sir John Cope, to mention a few. Cope wrote to a friend when he was abroad: 'Forget me not at Salter's in the next bowle.'

BISHOP—a fine old nightcap

'. . . Fine oranges,
Well roasted, with sugar and wine in a cup,
They'll make a sweet Bishop when gentlefolks sup.'

Dean Jonathan Swift, 1723.

2 small oranges	1-inch piece of cinnamon
8 cloves	2 pieces of blade mace
8 allspice berries or $\frac{1}{2}$ teaspoon	2 small pieces of ginger root
ground allspice	6 lumps of sugar rubbed over
$\frac{1}{2}$ pint (1 cup) (0·285 l.) water	the rind of a lemon
1 bottle port	a pinch of grated nutmeg

Stick the cloves into the oranges and either roast slowly in front of a slow fire, or bake in a pan in a slow oven for about 45 minutes. Put the cinnamon, mace, allspice, ginger root with the water into a saucepan and bring to the boil, then let it boil until it has reduced by about a third. Put the spices and water into a large warmed bowl with the roasted oranges and the sugar lumps rubbed over the lemon rind. Heat up the port, but do not let it boil, then pour over the fruit and spices. Stir well, then grate the nutmeg over the top and serve hot. Keep warm over a low flame but never let it boil.

Serves about 6-8.

Don Saltero's Coffee House, 18 Cheyne Walk, Chelsea, c. 1870; photographer, James Hedderley.

ROYAL CREAM, EUGENIES

The Great Exhibition of 1851 was the first of its kind ever to be held and both the idea and the organizing of it were due to Prince Albert's energy and ability. The Crystal Palace was erected in Hyde Park, then transferred to Sydenham. It promoted free trade and attracted world-wide attention. Many new ideas in food and eating came from the Exhibition, notably the picnic or transportable luncheon basket. This was first made by Scott's the London basketmakers for use at the Exhibition, and later it was used on trains, which at that time had no corridors or restaurant cars. It was also used by Victorians for eating out of doors, a favourite pastime. During the Risorgimento in Italy many Italians came to England and earned their living making ice-cream which was excellent and very different from the home-made, custard-based variety: these and jellies were all the rage with the visitors to the Exhibition, so much so that the price of hides used for making gelatine went up over 100 per cent. A current music-hall song warned people of the dangers of eating cold things when hot:

> *'All you who're fond, in spite of price,*
> *Of pastries, creams and jellies nice,*
> *Be cautious how you take to ice,*
> *Whenever you're over-warm!'*

Jacob Beuler

ROYAL CREAM

1¾ pints (3¼ cups) (1 l.) milk	8 egg-yolks
6 macaroons	½ lb. (1 cup) (227 gr.) vanilla
1 tablespoon gelatine	caster (fine) sugar
	¼ cup cold water

Soak the gelatine in cold water, then crush the macaroons to a fine powder. Beat the egg-yolks and sugar together well and add the macaroon powder. Bring the milk to the boil and pour over the egg mixture, stirring thoroughly. Fill a 3-pint (2-l.) mould with cold water and let it stand for a few minutes. Put the mixture in a saucepan or double boiler over a gentle heat and when it is smooth and coats the spoon evenly, take from the heat and stir in the gelatine, mixing well with a whisk. Empty the mould and pour in the cream, then chill. To unmould, wrap a hot cloth round the outside, put a dish over the top and turn quickly. Decorate with chopped, toasted almonds. If preferred the cream can be put into individual pots and served from them. *Serves 8.*

EUGENIES

4 oz. (1 cup) (113 gr.) ground almonds	4 oz. (½ cup) (114 gr.) sugar
1 tablespoon cold water	1 egg and 1 egg-yolk
1½ oz. (⅓ cup) (43 gr.) flour	1 tablespoon Curaçao or orange liqueur
½ teaspoon salt	vanilla sugar

Mix the ground almonds with half the sugar and the cold water, then add the remaining sugar and the beaten egg, mixing well with a wooden spoon. Add the egg-yolk, then the flour, salt and Curaçao, mixing each ingredient in very thoroughly. Beat for a few minutes, then put about a tablespoon in greased patty tins and bake in a moderate oven (375°F.) for 15 minutes. Dredge with vanilla sugar when cooked. *Makes about 12.*

Queen Victoria, Prince Albert, the Emperor Louis Napoleon and the Empress Eugénie at the Great Exhibition, Crystal Palace, 20th April, 1855.

ROAST PORK

ROAST PORK WITH APPLES AND RAISINS

One of the special delights of a joint of roast pork is the crisp and delicious crackling: that is, the skin on the outside. In order that this should be crisp and crunchy, the skin should never come into contact with the boiling fat during cooking, or it will fry and become as tough as leather. This crispness can be achieved either by placing the joint on a rack, or by the easier and better method of pouring about 1 inch of water into the roasting pan, and using no added fat for cooking. The fat from the meat drips into the water, and the steam tenderizes the joint. Also, once the excess fat is drained off, there is an excellent gravy in the pan.

1 leg or loin of pork about 5 lb. (2·250 kg.)	2 cups water (approx.)
8 medium-sized eating apples	1 cup mixed raisins and sultanas
salt and pepper	1 small sprig sage

Tuck the sage under the skin of the pork, or if fresh sage is not available rub powdered sage over the skin, and dust with salt and pepper. Put into a baking tin with the water and cook in a moderate oven (350°F.) for 30 minutes to the pound. Core the apples but do not peel them, and fill the centres with the mixed fruit; arrange these around the pork when it has been cooking for about $\frac{3}{4}$ hour, and bake them with the joint. When ready, pour off any excess fat and make a gravy by adding either a little water or cider to the pan juices, and reduce on top of the stove. Apple sauce is not necessary with this method, but a little crab-apple jelly, if available, is pleasant put on top of the apples before serving.

Serves 8.

ROAST PORK WITH ORANGE is another old English method with pork. Use large unpeeled oranges cut into quarters instead of the apples as above, and add them about 1 hour before the joint is cooked. Add a tablespoonful of crab-apple or red-currant jelly to the pan juices, also about 4 tablespoons sherry, and boil up as in previous recipe.

The Pre-Raphaelite painters and designers, Edward Burne-Jones and William Morris, with their families at Burne-Jones's house, The Grange, North End Road, Fulham, c. 1876. From left to right: Richard Burne-Jones (father of E. Burne-Jones), Margaret Burne-Jones, Edward Burne-Jones, Philip Burne-Jones, Mrs Burne-Jones, May Morris, William Morris, Mrs William Morris and Jenny Morris.

BAKED HAM À LA CAFÉ ROYAL, WITH CUMBERLAND SAUCE

The Café Royal was started by Daniel Nicolas Thevenon and his wife Celestine in 1865, a few years after Gatti's (page 27) had opened. He changed his name to Nicols, and this is why the plates and cutlery were stamped with an 'N', not because of Napoleon with whom he was, in fact, at loggerheads. First he opened a small café in Glasshouse Street, but a few years later expanded to the present premises. Its success was immediate and lasted for many decades. In 1867 Gustave Doré entertained his friend Giacomo Rossini there and it has always been well known and loved by all members of artistic or Bohemian society. Hardly a name of note from Oscar Wilde to Dylan Thomas has not enjoyed many a pleasant evening there.

'... I was inducted to another haunt of intellect and daring, the Domino Room of the Café Royal. There, on that October evening, there, in that exuberant vista of gilding, and crimson velvet, set amongst all those opposing mirrors and upholding caryatids, with fumes of tobacco ever rising to the painted and pagan ceiling, and with the hum of presumably cynical conversation broken into sharply now and again by the clatter of dominoes shuffled on marble tables, I drew a deep breath and "This indeed", I said to myself, "is life".'

Max Beerbohm, *c.* 1890s.

1 10-lb. (5-kg. approx.) ham, soaked overnight in cold water
½ lemon
24 cloves

6 tablespoons approx. brown sugar
½ bottle each, sherry and white wine

FOR THE SAUCE

This sauce should be made at least a day before, and will keep for months if airtight
1 lb. (2 cups) (454 gr.) redcurrant jelly
2 tablespoons Worcestershire sauce
grated rind and juice of

1 lemon and the same of
1 orange
½ bottle port
1 tablespoon Harvey sauce or mushroom ketchup (page 63)
1 tablespoon grated horseradish (optional)
12 glacé cherries (optional)

Scrape the skin of the soaked ham, and put into a large saucepan, with the lemon, and cover with cold water. Bring to the boil and simmer very gently for 1½ hours. Lift out and take off the skin. Cut shallow lattice marks all over the fat and stick a clove in each diamond, then pack on the brown sugar. Put into a baking tin with the wines and bake at 300°F. for about 1½-2 hours. When ready, reduce the juice on top of the stove and serve separately. It can be eaten hot or cold. Enough for about 20.

TO MAKE THE SAUCE, boil the jelly and port together until reduced by half. When cool add all other ingredients, the cherries cut in half. Put into jars and tie down. Serve cold, when it will be slightly jellied. Makes about 2 lb. (1 kg.)

The Café Royal, Regent Street, c. 1910.

CUPS, COCKTAILS AND GROGS

'A judicious mixer is not at all out of place on board a yacht . . . Not much is wanted in the way of paraphernalia. A very big jug or half-gallon mug, and a lump of ice, are, in fact, all the extras required. The sugar and lemon and the needful bottles take up very little room, and may even be classed as necessaries, and the skilful concoctor will want but little space and time to produce any of the following "coolers" . . .

'4 lumps of sugar to a bottle . . . of claret will be about the mark . . . Take 4 good-sized lumps of sugar and the peel of half a lemon cut very thin. Put these into your jug and add sufficient water (hot for choice) to cover the sugar. Let the sugar melt . . . cover the top of the jug if hot water is used, and then add a glass of sherry and half a glass of brandy. Put in as large a lump of ice as circumstances will admit of, and immediately add a bottle of claret and . . .two bottles of soda water. Then take out the lemon-peel, insert a handful of borage, a sprig of fresh mint, and a couple of thin slices of lemon, stir and drink. Some artists have a weakness for adding a piece of cucumber rind . . . good orange brandy may be safely used instead of brandy pure and simple . . . A bottle of lemonade and 1 of soda . . . have been used with success, especially if the party consist largely of ladies . . . the best variation is to leave out the brandy, decrease the quantity of sugar and add a bottle of champagne.

'*Cocktails* are easy to concoct with the assistance of 2 metal cups with a bevilled edge, to enable them to fit closely . . . Put into 1 of your cups a piece of thin lemon-peel, about 2 or 3 inches long, a little powdered sugar, a dash of bitters, and a half a glass of gin, whisky, or brandy, or a glass of sherry or claret. Fill up with small pieces or shavings of ice. Then fix on your other cup and shake . . . vigorously. Remove the top cup, add a good squeeze of lemon juice and rub the edge of your glass with the same . . . As Mr Bob Sawyer remarked "in its native pewter" is best. Champagne makes a capital cocktail, but will not stand the shaking up process . . . so add it last. Lemon, sugar, bitters, ice . . . a glass of good sherry, a spoonful of brandy and the yolk of an egg all shaken well up, make an excellent restorative . . . with fresh mint, 2 or 3 strawberries or raspberries, a slice of orange . . . '

'*Grogs* are simple matters . . . The following will be found a very good punch for a cold night, and if taken in sufficient quantities, will excite no painful reminiscences in the morning. First ascertain that the jug is perfectly clean and dry: yacht stewards are not to be trusted . . . any more than parlour-maids. Have the kettle on the fire before you . . . Into the jug put 5 lumps of sugar and the peel of a lemon cut then add a little boiling water, and cover your jug with a plate. While the stewing is going on, strain the juice of a lemon . . . and add in 5 minutes. Then add of wineglasses full of rum, gin or whisky, as many as you think discreet, and fill up with boiling water on the same principle. Take out the lemon-peel and swaddle the jug, all over in a piece of thick flannel . . . It is a pleasant nightcap. Some people add a liqueur even here, but that is a mistake to be carefully avoided . . . If the drink be wanted cold, add a lump of ice after the stewing, and proceed as afterwards, but with iced water.'   Charles Dickens, *Dictionary of the Thames*

Regatta Day on the Thames, c. *1890s.*

BAKED CUSTARD, WHIPPED LONDON SYLLABUB

The rapid expansion of London is pointed when one sees such an idyllic scene (in what is now such a busy thoroughfare) a mere sixty years ago. But it is even more stressed when one realizes that on the site of Earl's Court Station was a prosperous farm of 213 acres, owned by a Mr Hutchins. In 1888 W. J. Loftie in Kensington, Picturesque and Historical *wrote: 'The Manor House and land occupied by Mr Hutchins of Earl's Court Farm extended westwards as far as Kensington Canal (now West London Extension Railway). The road to Holland House formerly ran through the centre of the lands, planted with elms on each side, all of which have long since disappeared, but the land is still called Holland Walk.' In early Victorian times the village of Earl's Court consisted of a few houses and cottages, mostly on the eastern side of Earl's Court Road. On the western side were the farm and Manor House. North, south, east and west of the village lay open country, mainly farms and orchards. The expansion of the Earl's Court of today began in the late 1860s.*

BAKED CUSTARD

2 eggs	1 pint (2 cups) (0·57 l.) milk
2 egg-yolks	2 oz. (¼ cup) (57 gr.)
a little grated nutmeg	sugar

This custard is extremely pure and good in flavour, but if a stronger taste is required then add a little grated lemon or orange zest, brandy, vanilla, rosewater, orange flower water, almond etc. If using orange or lemon rind then infuse it in the milk while it is being heated and strain before adding to the eggs. This mixture can also be put into pastry cases and baked for 25 minutes in a moderate oven (350°F.) to make small custard tarts. Or if 4 oz. (½ cup) (113 gr.) sugar is heated and allowed to melt and colour without stirring, it can be rolled around a bowl, before adding the custard and when cooked and turned out when cold, it will be a Caramel Cream.

Put the sugar and milk into a saucepan and let the sugar melt, but do not let the milk boil. Beat the eggs and egg-yolks with a fork (too much beating makes the custard watery) in a large bowl, and then pour the milk over. Put into an ovenproof dish, grate nutmeg over the top and stand in a tin with hot water to half-way up and bake in a moderate oven (350°F.) for about 45 minutes, until the custard is set and the top slightly browned. It can be served warm or cold, and is often presented with stewed fruits.   Serves 4.

WHIPPED LONDON SYLLABUB

Adapted from Cassell's *Dictionary of Cookery,* 1877.

1 tablespoon sugar	a pinch of nutmeg
½ pint (1 cup) (0·285 l.)	1 pint (2 cups) (0·57 l.)
Madeira or sherry	cream

Mix together the sugar, wine and nutmeg, then divide this liquid between 4 or 6 long glasses and pour it into the bottom. Whip the cream and likewise divide this between the glasses, pouring it slowly on top of the wine mixture. Leave in a cool place for several hours or overnight, before serving.   For 4-6.

Feeding the chickens at Glover's Farm and Dairy, Brook Green Road (now Shepherd's Bush Road) Hammersmith, c. 1910. Glover's Farm was situated where the police station now is.

HOT TONGUE WITH CHERRY SAUCE

Hyde Park is one of the five large London parks, which originally were royal preserves, later given to the people. In the eighteenth century it was a favourite place for duels; the elder Pitt was the first to call the park 'the lungs of London'. Since Victorian times it has been a great place for open-air orators, and in 1872 a special place, now known as 'Speaker's Corner' was allotted for this purpose. Rotten Row is reserved for riders on horse-back, and in the old days carriages were also driven down it. The name is a corruption of Route du Roi.

HOT TONGUE WITH CHERRY SAUCE

Adapted from Lady Dudley's Book of Recipes, 1909.

1 4-lb. (1·814-kg.) salted ox or calf tongue*
1 large carrot
2 medium onions
3 cloves
8 peppercorns
a sprig of thyme and parsley

¼ pint (½ cup) (0·142 l.) port
¼ pint (½ cup) (0·142 l.) claret
juice of 3 medium oranges
juice of 1 lemon
1 tablespoon whole mango chutney
2 tablespoons tongue stock
1 tablespoon redcurrant jelly
black pepper
½ lb. (1 cup) (227 gr.) stoned, fresh, bottled or canned black cherries

*Pressure cooking time 1 hour

Soak the tongue overnight and trim off the horny and fatty parts. Put it into a large saucepan, cover with cold water and set to boil with the sliced carrot, onion stuck with cloves, peppercorns, thyme and parsley. Put the lid on, bring to the boil and simmer for about 3-4 hours, or until the tongue is tender. Let it cool slightly, remove from the stock and plunge into cold water. This makes it much easier to skin. Remove all skin and the root of the tongue, then put it back in the stock, and keep warm. Taste the stock for saltiness and if too salty, then do not use it in the sauce, but substitute water or white wine.

TO MAKE THE SAUCE, mix together the redcurrant jelly, port, claret, mango chutney, orange and lemon juice, stock and black pepper, and boil all together rapidly for ½ hour until it has reduced to almost half the quantity. Strain, and add the cherries. If the cherries are fresh, cook for 10 minutes and then serve the sauce over the hot tongue, cut into thick slices. If using canned or bottled cherries, they will only need heating up.

Serves about 6.

90

A stroll along Rotten Row, Hyde Park, 1912.

EGGS À LA ST JAMES'S

St James's Street has been known for famous London Clubs since the seventeenth century. The Thatched House (where the Conservative Club now stands) was a tavern where people interested in classical antiquities gathered. Swift wrote to Stella in 1711 of 'having entertained our Society at the Thatched House Tavern'. White's was a chocolate house in 1693 and became a club as we know it in 1736. It took its name from a steward employed there. Brooks' Club, founded in Pall Mall in 1764, moved to St James's Street in 1778 and like White's was famous for the gambling that took place. Boodle's was founded in 1763, and the Carlton Club, by the Duke of Wellington, in 1832. *See also pages 15, 61.*

EGGS À LA ST JAMES'S

8 eggs
1 tablespoon finely chopped
  parsley
1 tablespoon butter

8 slices of fried bread
  croûtons
cayenne pepper
salt
8 tinned anchovies

FOR THE SAUCE

1 pint (2 cups) (0·57 l.) milk
1 chopped shallot or button
  onion
1 tablespoon butter

small piece of blade mace
2 teaspoons anchovy essence
2 level tablespoons flour

First make the sauce by boiling the chopped shallot and mace in the milk until it is soft. Then melt the butter and stir in the flour, letting it cook for 1 minute. Add the strained milk and stir until the sauce is smooth, then add the anchovy essence and let it simmer gently. Butter eight small cocotte dishes liberally and press the parsley around the sides and dust with cayenne, break an egg into each one, taking care not to break the yolks, then either bake them in a hot oven (400°F.) for 15 minutes, or stand in a pan of boiling water to half way up, with a lid on, until the eggs are set but in no way hard. Ease with a knife round the edges and tip out onto the fried bread croûtons and pour the sauce around. Decorate with strips of tinned anchovy.

Serves 4 or 8. Served over potatoes or boiled rice, this makes a good luncheon dish.

ANGELS ON HORSEBACK

A Victorian savoury which consists of oysters rolled in rashers of streaky bacon which are then cooked under a hot grill or in a hot oven until the bacon is crisp. These rolls are then served on hot buttered toast. If cooking large numbers it is easier to thread them on a skewer. Allow at least 2 per person.

DEVILS ON HORSEBACK

12 pitted prunes stuffed with chopped mango chutney
6 rashers of bacon
1 tablespoon grated cheese   buttered bread

Roll up the stuffed prunes in the bacon rashers, place 2 on buttered bread and sprinkle with grated cheese. Cook in a hot oven (400°F.) or under a grill until the bacon is crisp. Or thread on skewers and serve on buttered toast. Allow at least 2 per person.

PIGEON PIE

'*Of all the quarters in the sheer adventurous amalgam called London, Soho is perhaps the least suited to the Forsyte spirit. Untidy, full of Greeks . . . cats, Italians, tomatoes, restaurants, organs, coloured stuffs, queer names, people looking out of windows . . .*'

John Galsworthy.

'. . . some pretty collation
Of Cheesecakes and Custards, and
Pidgeon-pye-puff,
With Bottle-Ale, Cider and
Such sort of stuff.' Ned Ward, *c.* 1835.

PIGEON PIE

This recipe can also be used for braising pheasants, partridge or grouse.

4 pigeons	4 large mushrooms
1 lb. (454 gr.) sausagemeat	1 pint (2 cups) (0·57 l.) stock
4 slices of ham	4 tablespoons sherry
1 medium sliced onion	a pinch of mace
2 bay leaves	salt and pepper
1 tablespoon parsley	
a pinch of thyme	
beurre manié of 1 tablespoon	
butter mixed with the same	
of flour	
½ lb. (227 gr.) puff pastry (page 113)	
or shortcrust pastry (page 109)	

Put the pigeons into a large saucepan with thyme, parsley, salt and pepper, pour over the stock, cover and simmer gently for about ½ hour. Let them cool slightly, then pick all the meat from the bones. Put the bones back into the stock, add half the quantity of water, season to taste and boil up gently for about ½ hour. Meanwhile take a large deep pie-dish and line the bottom and sides with the sausagemeat which has been seasoned and mixed with thyme and parsley. On top put a bay leaf, a layer of the pigeon meat, half the mushrooms, half the onion and 2 slices of ham. Repeat from the bay leaf, ending with the remaining ham slices. Strain the stock, add the pinch of mace, and stir in the *beurre manié*, then boil until it thickens slightly and is reduced. Add the sherry, and pour into the pie-dish, very gently from the sides until the liquid comes to about ½ inch from the top. Damp the edges of the pie-dish and press down the pastry, making a small cut on top to let out the steam. Brush over with beaten egg or milk, and bake in a moderate oven (350°F.) for about 1 hour. If the pastry appears to be getting too brown, then cover the top with a sheet of foil. This pie can be served hot or cold. If serving cold, then add 1 tablespoon aspic powder to the stock, so that it jells.

Serves 6-8.

This can also be made as a raised pie (page 71); and if served without a pastry crust but cooked with a lid on, it is known as a Compote of Pigeons.

The Watcher from the Window, Soho, 1903.

WINE JELLY, BRANDIED PEACHES

Belgravia, which covers roughly Belgrave, Lowndes and Eaton Squares with the streets radiating from them, consisted of open fields and small coppices in the eighteenth century. Thomas Cubitt laid out and built the present day Belgravia under an Act of Parliament passed in 1826.

> *'Belgravia! that fair spot of ground*
> *Where all that worldlings covet most, is found!*
> *Of this stupendous town—this mighty heart*
> *Of England's frame—the fashionable part.'*
>
> Mrs Gascoigne.

The 'social round' at this time was extremely fatiguing, thus many innocuous dishes were well fortified with alcohol to keep the spirit from flagging.

WINE JELLY

½ pint (1 cup) (0·285 l.) port*
½ pint (1 cup) (0·285 l.) water
1 tablespoon redcurrant jelly

2 oz. (¼ cup) (57 gr.) powdered glucose or sugar
rind and juice of 1 lemon
½ oz. (1 rounded tablespoon)
(14 gr.) gelatine

*Red wine, Madeira, Maraschino etc., can also be used.

Wash and peel the lemon thinly and strain the juice from it. Put all ingredients except the port into a rinsed pan and stir over heat, until gelatine and jelly are dissolved. Draw pan to one side and infuse for 15 minutes. Add the port, strain and pour into six small individual dishes.

Serves 6.

This excellent jelly can also be made, and layered in a bowl with fresh strawberries, raspberries, peaches, or other soft fruits.

BRANDIED PEACHES

Apricots, cherries or large plums can also be used.

12 large peaches
1 lb. (2 cups) (454 gr.) sugar

1 pint (2 cups) (0·57 l.)
water
approx. ¾ pint (1½ cups)
(0·427 l.) brandy

The peaches may be left with the stones inside, or cut in half and the stones removed, according to taste. First put them into a large bowl and cover with boiling water, leave for a few minutes, then lift out carefully and remove the skin. Put the sugar and water into a saucepan, bring slowly to the boil so that the sugar dissolves, then boil rapidly until it is clear (230°F.), skimming if necessary. Let it get cold, then add an equal amount of brandy. Pack the peaches into wide-necked jars with either a screw-top or clip covers. Stir up the syrup and brandy and pour over, seeing that they are covered completely. Leave for 3 months if possible.

Makes about three 3-lb. jars.

'The Finishing Touches', Belgrave Square, 1903.

CHELSEA BUNS

'Dacre and Danvers, Steele and Sloane,
Swift for its air, and Mead for its tone,
Bishop and Duchess, Wit and Drone
With one consent came hither;
Holbein, Erasmus, Gorges and Bray,
Walpole and Smollett, Johnson, Gay,
Cheyne and Newton, each in his day
Loved Chelsea by the River.'

By Chelsea Reach, *R. Blunt*

'Prelates and princes, and lieges and Kings,
Hail for the bellman, who tinkles and sings,
Bouche of the highest and lowliest ones
There's a charm in the sound which nobody shuns,
Of "smoking hot, piping hot, Chelsea Buns"'!

The Old Chelsea Bun House, which sold as many as a quarter of a million buns in one day, was in fact in the Pimlico Road, and the old building was destroyed in 1839. It was run by a Mr Richard Hand and his family, and he was always known as 'Captain Bun'. He wore a long dressing-gown and a Turkish fez. On Sundays crowds would stream out to the Bun House, which was opposite Stromboli House and Pleasure Gardens. The Bun House also had a museum of freaks, a craze current in the eighteenth century. George III and Queen Charlotte were fond of driving out to the Bun House and would sit on the veranda munching buns to the delight of the curious crowd. He gave 'Captain Bun' a half gallon silver mug with five guineas in it. Chelsea Buns are now being made and sold again.

1¼ lb. (5 cups) (567 gr.) sifted, warmed flour
5 oz. (½ cup and 1 heaped tablespoon) (141 gr.) butter
5 oz. (½ cup and 1 heaped tablespoon) (141 gr.) caster (fine) sugar
1 oz. (28 gr.) yeast creamed with 1 teaspoon of sugar
4 eggs
¼ pint (½ cup) (0·142 l.) tepid milk
1 teaspoon mixed spice
4 oz. (1 cup) (113 gr.) currants
a pinch of salt
SYRUP FOR GLAZING
2 oz. (¼ cup) (57 gr.) sugar boiled with 2 tablespoons water.

Mix together the flour, salt and half the sugar, then rub half the butter into this mixture. Cream the yeast with the teaspoon of sugar, then add the tepid milk and the beaten eggs, mix well and pour this into a well in the centre of the flour. Mix well and knead until smooth. Cover and put to rise in a warm place for about 1½-2 hours and it is doubled in size. Soften the remaining butter by creaming, turn out the dough onto a floured board and knead lightly, then roll out to a square about ½ inch thick. Spread the creamed butter and half the remaining sugar, over, fold and roll out again. Sprinkle with the rest of the sugar, currants and spice, and roll up like a Swiss Roll. Cut into slices about 1½ inch thick and lay them close together on a warm, greased tin, and let them prove for 20 minutes. The buns should now be touching. Bake in a hot oven (400°F.) for about 30 minutes. Brush over with the glazing syrup, put back to dry and leave to cool before separating.   Makes about 12.

Boats on Chelsea Reach, The Pier Hotel in background, c. 1858.

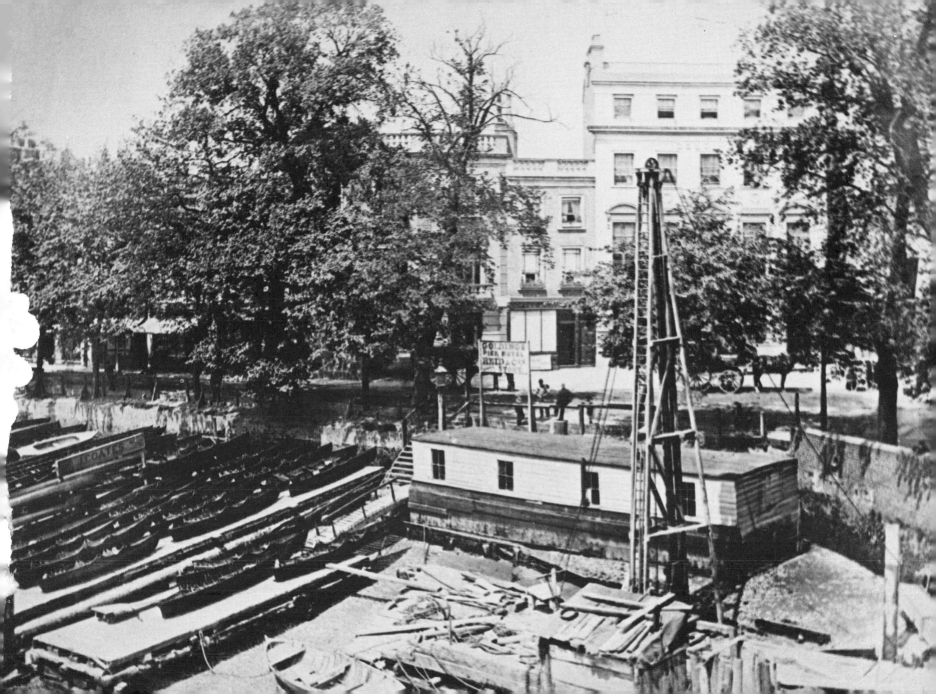

ARNOLD BENNETT OMELETTE

Henekey's still carries on today, looking little different from the photograph. The First Avenue Hotel whose table d'hote *cost 1s. 6d. in 1901 and consisted of : soup, fish, entrée or poultry, vegetables, ice and cheese, plus wine and coffee 2s. 6d., has gone, as has the nearby Cecil Hotel. Both catered for American visitors to London. The Strand Palace Hotel and the famous Savoy Hotel now dominate the hotel scene in the Strand.*

ARNOLD BENNETT OMELETTE

This was a favourite of the writer Arnold Bennett, and when he was a theatre critic he often had it at the Savoy Hotel after the theatre.

1 cup (170 gr.) cooked smoked haddock	1 teaspoon butter
6 eggs	2 tablespoons grated cheese, Parmesan for preference
3 tablespoons heavy cream	salt and pepper

Flake the boned, cooked fish and mix with the grated cheese and season to taste. Be wary of the salt for the fish and cheese might be very salty. Beat the eggs lightly, and melt the butter in a heavy frying pan. See that the stove is hot, but do not let the butter brown. Pour in the eggs and move them about with a slice once or twice, tipping the pan so that the eggs run all over it. When the bottom is set put the fish and cheese on top, let it get warm, and the omelette golden brown underneath. Do not let the top eggs set, they must still be creamy and liquid. Pour over the thick cream, sprinkle with freshly ground pepper and put under a hot grill for 2 minutes, or until the top is golden. Do not attempt to fold this omelette: it is made Spanish style, and is slid, cream side up, on to a hot plate. Serve with crusty bread or rolls and a tossed green salad.

Enough for 2.

Henekey's Wine and Spirit House, 354 Strand, c. 1890.

CLAIRS

This teashop, the first of many, was opened in 1894, and Lyons became famous for its cheerful and quick waitresses, known as 'Nippies'. In 1923 Lyons were the first to market the American-manufactured ice-cream block; previously ice-cream had been sold in wafers, or cornets, by mainly Italian travelling salesmen with a decorated stall or cart. Lyons sold not only cakes and tea, but also snacks, such as Welsh Rarebit or baked beans on toast. However, in the early days it was the thing for the middle classes to 'go to Joe Lyons for tea'. By far the most popular cakes were the éclair and cream bun.

ECLAIRS OR CREAM BUNS

4 oz. (1 cup) (113 gr.) plain	3 eggs
flour	¼ pint (½ cup) (0·142 l.)
2 oz. (¼ cup) (57 gr.) butter	water

Use a large enough saucepan to allow the eggs to be beaten in. Put the butter and water in the saucepan and bring to the boil, and when bubbling draw aside and immediately add the flour, all at once. Beat with a wooden spoon until smooth and the paste leaves the side of the pan cleanly. Cool slightly and meanwhile whisk the eggs lightly and add by degrees, beating thoroughly each time some is added. When all the eggs have been put in and the paste ready it should be smooth and shiny-looking. Put into a forcing bag with a half-inch tube and force on to a lightly greased baking tin (or use a spoon), to about 3½ inches long, or round if for cream buns, and not too close together. Then bake in a moderately hot oven (400°F.) for 30-35 minutes or until dry. Remove from the tray and slit down the side, then leave on a rack to cool. When cool they can be filled with whipped cream, and iced.

Makes 10 large, or 36 bite size.

TO ICE THE ÉCLAIRS. Chocolate or mocha is the usual icing. Cream buns are not iced but sprinkled with icing sugar.

4 oz. (1 cup) (113 gr.) icing	hot black coffee
(confectioner's) sugar	2 tablespoons melted butter
2 tablespoons cocoa	

Mix sugar, cocoa and butter together and moisten with hot coffee until it is the correct spreading consistency. Dip knife in the coffee while spreading over the buns. Alternatively 2 oz. (57 gr.) of dark block chocolate can be used with ½ cup (0·142 l.) milk, both heated until the chocolate melts and is cooled. Then beat in the butter and as much sugar as it will take to get spreading consistency.

These buns or éclairs without icing can be filled with savoury mixtures, such as creamed cottage cheese mixed with herbs, or smoked salmon; or mashed sardines; mashed hard-boiled eggs and cheese, or anchovies etc.

It is interesting to note that the first Indian tea was not sold in Britain until about 1830 (before that it was all China tea): in 1847 John Cassell (later to found Cassell's publishing house in 1850), then a tea and coffee merchant, gave away large quantities of India tea to the London poor in an attempt to stop the terrific amount of cheap alcoholic liquor which was then drunk by men and women. Its success was immediate.

The first Lyons Teashop, Piccadilly, c. 1900.

PRAWNS

The London Docks, which covered a land area of sixty acres and a water area of forty acres, were opened in 1805, but were closed in 1968 owing to new methods of cargo handling and the larger size of modern ships. These are now being accommodated at Tilbury and other docks in London. London dockland has a very polyglot population which is reflected in the cosmopolitan clientele of the pubs and the variety of food, such as the excellent Cantonese restaurant, 'Young Friends' just off the West India Dock Road, whose specialities are sweet and sour mullet and giant prawns.

PRAWNS IN BATTER WITH SWEET AND SOUR SAUCE

2 lb. (approx. 1 kg.) large prawns
8 oz. (2 cups) (227 gr.) flour
½ pint (1 cup) (0·285 l.) tepid water
2 tablespoons oil
2 stiffly beaten egg-whites
a pinch of salt
deep-fryer of oil

If the prawns are raw and still in their shells, then steam them over boiling water for 15 minutes, let them cool and remove the shells. To make the batter, mix the flour, oil and salt together, then add the tepid water and beat to a smooth paste. It will seem a bit thick, but that is as it should be. If the prawns are very large then cut them in half, and add the stiffly beaten egg-whites to the batter and mix well. Have ready the deep fryer of oil with the basket, and get the oil hot enough so that if a small piece of bread is dipped in it sizzles up and turns golden.

Dip the prawns in the batter, one at a time, and put into the hot oil about 3 or 4 at a time depending on the size of the basket. Turn when golden on one side and do the other. Lift out and drain. They will puff up a lot, and if only cooked until pale gold, they can be reheated, before serving at a later time. Drain and pile on to a hot dish. Batter left over can be stored in a screwtop jar for a few days in a cool place.

SWEET AND SOUR SAUCE

¼ pint (½ cup) (0·142 l.) vinegar
¼ pint (½ cup) (0·142 l.) water
2 tablespoons sugar and 1 tablespoon honey (or all sugar)
1 teaspoon soy sauce
½ teaspoon paprika
1 tablespoon cornflour (cornstarch)

Combine all ingredients except the cornflour in a saucepan and gently bring to the boil. Cream the cornflour with a little water and add to the mixture, stirring until it thickens. If too thick, add a little more vinegar and water mixed, until you have the right consistency. Hand soy sauce separately.

Serves 4.

The above batter can also be used for scallops, lobster, or chunks of thick white fish such as turbot. Likewise cubes of pork, brains etc.

Shipping entrance to London Dock, c. 1856.

BREAD AND BUTTER PUDDING

Not only has the quality of our daily bread deteriorated, but also the extremely smart turn-out of the driver, horse and cart, all of whom look as if they are ready for a day at Ascot. Bread, which was the basic fare for so many people, was delivered to the door, hot, and crusty, and in time for breakfast.

Bread and Butter Pudding is nowadays usually a nursery dish, but in the last century, well-laced with brandy or rum, it was considered the perfect follow-on after a brace of partridges, or some other rich dish.

½ pint (1 cup) (0·285 l.) milk
finely grated zest of ½ lemon
2 beaten eggs
a pinch of grated nutmeg
3 tablespoons sugar
2 tablespoons brandy, rum or
    sweet sherry

6 thickly buttered slices of
    crustless bread
2 tablespoons seedless raisins
    or sultanas, or a mixture
1 tablespoon chopped
    candied peel
a little butter

Butter a 3-pint (1½-l.) ovenproof dish and cover the bottom with 2 buttered bread slices. Sprinkle over a third of the sugar, then the same of the dried fruit and peel. Repeat this until these ingredients are used up, ending with a layer of bread, but not using the last of the sugar until later. Pour over the brandy. Make the custard by beating the eggs, then heating milk and lemon zest until it comes to the boil. Pour this over the eggs, stirring well, and pour this custard, not *over* the bread mixture but at the side of the dish. If possible leave to stand for about 1 hour, then sprinkle the top with the remaining sugar and nutmeg, then bake in a moderate oven (350°F.) for about 40 minutes, or until the top is well-browned and crusty, and the custard set. Serve hot from the dish.

Serves 4-6.

BROWN BREAD ICE CREAM
This was a favourite Victorian and Edwardian ice cream, and is extremely good. The brown breadcrumbs give the ice cream a nutty flavour, and I have often used them in a bought vanilla ice, first sprinkling them with sugar and crisping them for about 10 minutes in a moderate oven, then cooling, beating them into the ice cream and refreezing.

4 egg-yolks
2 tablespoons sugar
¾ pint (1½ cups) (approx. ½ l.)
    milk
1 tablespoon sherry, brandy or
    rum

¼ pint (½ cup) (0·142 l.)
    cream
2 oz. (1¼ cups) (57 gr.) stale
    brown breadcrumbs

Beat together the egg-yolks and the sugar, and put into a double boiler. Heat the milk and pour over gradually, stirring all the time. Let it cook over hot water until it thickens slightly, enough to coat the back of a spoon, then add the sherry, rum or brandy. Leave to cool. Meanwhile whip the cream, then add it to the mixture and finally the breadcrumbs. Put into a dish, and either chill, or freeze.

Serves 4.

See also Bread Sauce, page 111.

Chibnall's Bread Carts, Hammersmith, c. 1900.

BEEF STEW WITH ORANGE

Blackfriars gets its name from the black habits of the Dominican friars who came to London in 1221 and were given land there for their priory by Hubert de Burgh. After the Dissolution, one of the first theatres was made out of rooms in the priory in 1577, and in 1608 Richard Burbage, the famous tragedian, operated it as a playhouse with seven equal shareholders, one of whom was William Shakespeare. It was the winter home of the company, the Globe theatre being used in summer. Many of Shakespeare's plays were performed there. The Surrey Gardens and Music Hall were also in the vicinity.

2½ lb. (1 kg.) stewing steak	a sprig each of thyme and
2 tablespoons oil or dripping	parsley, chopped
10 button onions or 2 large	pinch of powdered marjoram
sliced	1 pint (2 cups) (0·57 l.) stock
1 tablespoon flour	1 chopped head celery
¼ pint (½ cup) (0·142 l.)	1 tablespoon finely shredded
red wine	orange peel
2 bay leaves	salt and pepper

Remove any fat, bone or gristle from the meat and cut into squares. Heat the oil in a metal casserole and fry the meat on both sides until brown. Remove the meat and fry the onions, whole if using the small ones, until they are golden. Dust in the flour and then add the red wine, meat, chopped celery, herbs and bay leaves, then pour over the stock and the orange peel. Season well, cover, and cook in a slow oven (275°F.) for about 1½ hours or until the meat is tender. Add a very little more liquid if it appears to be getting too dry. Dark beer can be used instead of wine if preferred.

Serves 4.

This stew makes an excellent basis for a steak pie: there are several variations which can be made, such as ½ lb. (227 gr.) button mushrooms instead of the celery, and the addition of ½ lb. (227 gr.) chopped ox kidney. When cooked, put the meat into a deep pie-dish and cover with shortcrust pastry.

SHORTCRUST PASTRY

8 oz. (2 cups) (227 gr.) self-	4 oz. (½ cup) (114 gr.)
raising flour	margarine, or margarine
a pinch of salt	and lard mixed
approx. 4 tablespoons water	

Mix the flour and salt together, then rub in the fat with the fingers, or use a pastry blender until the mixture is like fine breadcrumbs. Add the cold water gradually, using a knife or blender until the dough is soft and pliable, neither crumbly or slack. Turn out on to a floured board and roll to size required. Leave to stand in a cold place for 1 hour before using if possible. Damp the edges of the pie-dish then lay on the pastry, pressing down the edges. Brush over with milk or egg to glaze and make a nick in the top to let out steam. Bake in a hot oven (400°F.) for the first 10 minutes, then lower the heat to 325°F. until it is golden brown.

STUFFED ROAST TURKEY WITH BREAD SAUCE

1 hen turkey about 14 lb. (6½ kg.)
1 lb. (454 gr.) sausagemeat
5 tablespoons good poultry dripping
2 tablespoons butter
1 tablespoon redcurrant jelly
1 lb. (454 gr.) sausages
1 lemon
2 cups giblet stock

FOR THE STUFFING
4 oz. (2 cups) (113 gr.)
   breadcrumbs or 8 slices
   crustless bread
6 oysters, fresh or canned
   (optional)
8 large cooked chestnuts
1 small chopped celery heart
¼ pint (½ cup) (0·142 l.) milk
chopped raw turkey liver
1 teaspoon chopped parsley
salt and pepper

FOR THE SAUCE
2 cups white breadcrumbs
1 medium onion
4 cloves
a pinch of mace
6 peppercorns
½ pint (1 cup) (0·285 l.) milk
1 teaspoon butter
2 tablespoons cream
salt and pepper

To make the stuffing, soak the breadcrumbs in the milk until they have absorbed all the liquid, then combine all other ingredients, and stuff into the body of the bird and secure with a skewer. Now put as much of the sausagemeat into the crop end as it will take, and make the remainder into small balls. Put the bird into a roasting pan, brush all over with melted butter and put the dripping around. Cover with foil, and roast in a moderate oven (350°F.) for 20-25 minutes to the pound, lowering the heat to 300°F. after the first ½ hour. Baste frequently during cooking, and when half-cooked sprinkle with a little flour, salt and pepper. When cooked, pour off the excess fat, and put the bird on to a warmed dish and keep warm. Add 2 cups of giblet stock to the pan juices, the redcurrant jelly and season to taste. Boil up on the top of the stove, to reduce, and serve separately.

TO MAKE THE SAUCE
Stick the cloves into the onion and put into a saucepan with the milk, mace and peppercorns. Bring to the boil and then draw aside and let it infuse for ½ hour. Strain the milk into another saucepan and add the breadcrumbs. Stir until it is boiling, and quite thick. Season to taste and finally stir in the butter and cream. Do not reboil after this, and serve hot.

While the turkey is cooking and about ½ hour before it is ready, prick the sausages and fry them until brown and cooked through, then add the forcemeat balls and cook them until brown. Garnish the bird with the sausages, forcemeat balls and slices of lemon.

Serves about 8-10.

Interior of Leonard Jolly's provision store, 24 King Street, Hammersmith, 1910.

ALMOND CHEESECAKES

'*So abroad with my wife, in the afternoon, to the Park, where very much company, and the weather very pleasant. I carried my wife to the Lodge, the first time this year, and there in our coach eat a cheesecake and drank a tankard of milk.*'

25th April, 1669, Samuel Pepys.

The Lodge was a cake-house in Hyde Park, a favourite place for a rendezvous well into the nineteenth century. There is still a small café for tea and cakes in nearby Kensington Gardens.

'The almond cheesecakes will be always hot at 1 o'clock as usual; and the rich seed and plum-cakes sent to any part of the town at 2/6d. each. Coffee, tea and chocolate at any time of the day; and fine Epping butter may also be had.'

Advertisement in the *Daily Advertiser*, 6th May, 1760, by Mr Trusler, Marylebone Gardens.

Almond Cheesecakes are very similar to 'Maids of Honour', small cakes reputed to have been first made at the court of Henry VIII. They are still sold in many cake shops in Richmond, where they are famous.

FOR THE PUFF PASTRY

12 oz. (3 cups) (340 gr.) flour	7-8 tablespoons iced water
12 oz.(1½ cups) (340 gr.) butter	a pinch of salt

FOR THE FILLING

4 oz. (1 cup) (113 gr.) ground almonds	3 egg-yolks
4 tablespoons melted butter	2 tablespoons sugar
¼ pint (½ cup) (0·142 l.) cream or top of the milk	juice and rind of 1 lemon or orange

First make the pastry by stirring the salt into the flour in a basin. Then rub in half the butter and add enough water to make a firm dough. Turn out on to a floured board and roll to a rectangle about ½-inch thick. Add the remaining butter, in little pieces, on to half the dough, then fold over, envelope fashion, pressing the edges well together. Let it stand for 10 minutes. With the sealed end towards you, roll away from you: then fold the dough into three, and turn around again so that the open edge faces you, then roll again. Repeat this twice more, so that the pastry has six turns of rolling and resting and has no streaks of butter in it. Keep everything as cold as possible, and store in a cold place until you need it. Then roll out on a lightly floured board and cut into shapes to fit lightly greased patty tins or small cake-tins.

To prepare the filling, finely grate the lemon or orange rind and squeeze out the juice. Mix with the almonds, melted butter, egg-yolks, sugar and finally the cream. Pour into the pastry cases and cook in a moderate oven (350°F.) for about 15 minutes, or until they are golden brown. Serve cold.

Makes about 24.

Conversation Piece at Hyde Park Corner, c. 1885.

COMPOTE OF FRUIT

Among the street-folk there are many distinct characters of people—people differing as widely from each other in tastes, habits thoughts and creed, as one nation from another. Of these the costermongers form by far the largest and certainly the most broadly marked class. They appear to be a distinct race—perhaps originally of Irish extraction—seldom associating with any other of the street-folks, and all being known to each other.'

Henry Mayhew, London Labour and the London Poor, *1851*

In the 1850s more than half the apples and pears reaching Covent Garden and the other metropolitan vegetable markets were taken by costers. In all about £2 million worth of food was sold on the London streets, the lion's share of it by fully fledged costermongers. They were easily recognized by their flashy dress, usually a velveteen or corduroy longish jacket with brass, pearl or carved buttons. (The Pearly Kings came about only in their decline, when they had become a butt for music-hall performers.) A large silk handkerchief, known as a 'Kingsman' was tied around the throat, by both men and women. They had a slang language of their own, and at that time only about one-tenth of the couples living together were married. Their amusements were '2d. hops' (dances), the theatre and the penny concert. Their visits were confined to the south-side, the halls they favoured being the Surrey, the Victoria, the Coburg (Old Vic) and the Bower Saloon. Three times a week was the average attendance at theatres and dances by the prosperous ones. 'Love and murder suits us best, sir . . .'

Compote of Fruit, a Victorian and Edwardian dish which was often served with a milk pudding or, when oranges were used, as a side dish for chestnut purée, or chocolate mousse. Almost all fruits (or a mixture) can be used, but it is essential that whatever is selected is lightly poached in syrup, not water.

The amount of sugar used depends upon the acidity of the fruit: green gooseberries, rhubarb etc., allow 10 oz. ($1\frac{1}{4}$ cups) (284 gr.) sugar to $\frac{1}{2}$ pint water; apricots, strawberries, raspberries, cherries etc., 6 oz. ($\frac{3}{4}$ cup) (170 gr.) is enough, although the ripeness of the fruit must be taken into consideration.

Boil the sugar with the water for about 15 minutes, letting it boil rapidly when the sugar has melted. Let the syrup cool, for some hours if possible, then gently poach the fruit (1 lb. (454 gr.) for above quantity) until it is just soft, but not mushy. If using oranges, they can be easily peeled if first steeped in boiling water for about $\frac{1}{2}$ hour: or they may be thinly sliced through with the peel, which acquires a pleasant flavour and texture after the poaching. Reserve the peel of at least 1 orange, and pare it into fine strings over the top of the compote. In all cases a little spirit or liqueur added to taste, is very acceptable.

GRAPE JELLY is another pretty Victorian idea. Select a bunch of seedless grapes on the stalk. Immerse them in wine jelly (page 97), seeing that they are kept straight by hanging them by string from a nail. When set, cut down, and turn it all out. It makes an attractive centre piece.

Costermonger with his fruit barrow outside the National Gallery, Trafalgar Square, c. 1916.

MR GAY'S RECEIPT TO STEW A KNUCKLE OF VEAL

from *The Cook's Oracle*, by Dr Kitchiner, 1817.

Lawrence Street is one of the oldest in Chelsea : Monmouth House (formerly Lawrence House) was built by Thomas Lawrence, a goldsmith, in 1544. A later Lady Lawrence rented the house to the Duchess of Monmouth, and John Gay (author of The Beggar's Opera*) became her secretary for a short time in 1714, but after a few months wrote to Swift, 'I am quite off from the Duchess of Monmouth's'. The next tenant was Tobias Smollett in 1749. About this time Chelsea became a favourite place for thousands of people to go to on Sundays. This prompted Gay to write the following rhyme :*

> *'Then Chelsey's meads o'erhear perfidious vows,*
> *And the press'd grass defrauds the grazing cows.'*

In 1711 Swift wrote in his Journal :

'June 19th. Do you know that about our town [Chelsea] we are mowing already and making hay and it smells so sweet as we walk through the flowering meads; but the haymaking nymphs are perfect drabs, nothing so clean and pretty as further in the country. There is a mighty increase of dirty wenches in straw hats since I knew London.'

'Take a knuckle of Veal;
You may buy it, or steal:
In a few pieces cut it,
In a stewingpan put it;
Salt, pepper and mace,
Must season this knuckle;

Then, what's joined to a place *
With other herbs muckle;
That which kill'd King Will **
And what never stands still; ***
Some sprigs of that bed ****
Where children are bred,
Which much you will mend, if
Both spinage and endive,
And lettuce and beet,
With marygold meet,
Put no water at all,
For it maketh things small,
Which lest it should happen,
A close cover clap on:
Put this pot of Wood's metal *****
In a boiling hot kettle;
And there let it be,
(Mark the doctrine I teach)
About, let me see,
Thrice as long as you preach. ******
So skimming the fat off,
Say Grace with your hat off,
O! then with what rapture
Will it fill Dean and Chapter!'

* celery ** supposed sorrel *** thyme (time) **** parsley
**** an alloy of exceptionally low melting point.
***** which we suppose to be near four hours.

Corner of Lawrence Street and Cheyne Walk, Chelsea, c. 1870 ; photographer, James Hedderley.

THE LONDON PARTICULAR (Pea soup)

The Canterbury Music Hall was started in 1849 by Charles Morton, who lived to be called the 'Father of the Halls'. It was called the Canterbury Arms or Hall until the early twentieth century; at the back of the tavern he built a new hall where the concerts were held. The entrance fee was a 6d. 'Refreshment ticket' which entitled the holders to see the show, and use the bars, and skittle alleys. He endeared himself to the ladies by providing the first weekly 'Ladies' Night'. In 1856 he built on an annexe where he exhibited paintings by contemporary artists, such as Maclise, Frith, Bonheur, etc. In 1867 he gave up the management to devote himself to the newly opened Oxford Hall. The Canterbury was completely rebuilt by the 1890s with a stage and seats as in a theatre, whereas in the old days the main hall had long tables with chairs running the length of the auditorium, facing the raised platform at the end. The new Canterbury had a long bar at the back with a window, which you could see through and decide whether you wanted to drink or see the show. The performance started at 7.30 p.m. and some twenty or twenty-five acts were performed. The building in the photograph was blitzed in 1940.

'A well-lighted entrance attached to a public-house indicates that we have reached our destination. We proceed up a few stairs . . . where we pay sixpence if we take a seat in the body of the hall and 9d. if we ascend to the gallery. We make our way . . . to the floor of the hall, which is well-lighted and capable of holding 1,500 people. A balcony extends around . . . at the opposite end is a platform on which are placed a grand piano and a harmonium on which the performers play in the intervals when the previous singers have left the stage. . . .'

J. E. Richie, in The Night Side of London, *1857.*

'". . . this is a London particular." . . . "A fog miss," said the young gentleman.' Charles Dickens, *Bleak House*. Subsequently a dense London fog became known as a 'pea-souper'.

1 lb. (2 cups) (454 gr.) split green peas, soaked overnight (whole dried peas can be used)
1 large sliced onion
4 rashers bacon, or a ham-bone
4 pints (8 cups) (2¼ l.) water, or preferably stock from ham, tongue or salt beef, but taste for saltiness before using
1 tablespoon Worcestershire sauce
2 tablespoons cream for garnish (optional)
small croûtons of fried bread   salt and pepper

Soak the dried peas for at least 4 hours and preferably overnight. Cut the bacon into dice (or use a well-covered hambone) and let the fat run out in a large saucepan, then lightly fry the onion in it until just soft. Add the peas, water or stock, cover and simmer for about 2 hours or until the peas are puréed. Carrots or a stalk of celery can also be added, but are not strictly traditional. If using whole dried peas and they do not go to a purée, they can be liquidized or put through a food mill. Stir well, and taste for seasoning, then add the Worcestershire sauce, and heat up. Before serving, stir in the cream, or float it on top, and serve with small ½-inch fried bread croûtons. If any is left over it can be reheated if more stock or milk is added first, but heat it gently, lest it burn.

This soup can be pressure-cooked. Time, once the pressure has been reached, is 35 minutes.   Serves about 6-8.

The last night at the Canterbury Music Hall, Lambeth, May, 1912.

INDEX